30 Holiday Patterns for Carvers

Al Streetman

Schiffer Publishing Ltd

4880 Lower Valley Road, Atglen, PA 19310

Dedication

To all my readers ... without your support, I would have never made it this far. I thank you all.

Acknowledgments

The following people helped make this book possible. I thank you all:

Jody Garrett, Woodcraft Supply Corporation: For all the help you give to us "starving artists," and for providing us with various carving tool samples for evaluation and consideration.

DecoArt: The paint samples were excellent--satisfactory in all respects.

Woodcraft Supply Corporation: Parkersburg, West Virginia: For the high-quality carving tools and supplies.

Royal Brush Mfg., Inc.: Excellent quality paintbrushes at an affordable price.

Catalog Card Number: 97-81075

Designed by Laurie A. Smucker
Typeset in Times New Roman/Bookman Old

ISBN: 0-7643-0514-X
Printed in China

Published by Schiffer Publishing Ltd.
4880 Lower Valley Road
Atglen, PA 19310
Phone: (610) 593-1777; Fax: (610) 593-2002
E-mail: schifferbk@aol.com
Please write for a free catalog.
This book may be purchased from the publisher.
Please include $3.95 for shipping.
Try your bookstore first.

We are interested in hearing from authors with book ideas on related subjects.

Table of Contents

Introduction

For authors, one of the most difficult challenges we face is trying to come up with new ideas for books. We have lots of ideas, but it requires many of these ideas to be logically connected in order to acquire enough material to develop into a book. This book is in response to your requests for more (and various) patterns such as Santas, leprechauns, etc. This book is a compilation of new patterns which should provide something to carve for most every major holiday or holiday season.

Since Santa is an ever-popular character, and many people are keeping Santas out year-round as part of their home decor, I chose a simple and easy-to-carve Santa for the project in this book. Future books I write in this same manner will feature other characters for the carving project such as Uncle Sam, a leprechaun, an angel, etc.

Some of you may observe that my carving project is not as complex or detailed as you might carve it. There is a method to my madness. In this book, as in my previous books, I have tried to design a project that would yield a nice result, yet not be so complex or involved that the *beginning wood carver* would not be able to accomplish it. I want to reach as many wood carvers as possible, and share the joy of carving with them. As the beginners gain more experience, they can add additional details as desired.

Except for the actual carving project, I have not included specific carving instructions. I have found that each carver has his or her own style and each has their own tool preference for use in a particular area, or to achieve a particular effect.

Rather than giving a vague instruction such as "use a small gouge," I have listed the particular size tool I used in the different steps of the carving project, as we move through each step of the carving. This is more for the benefit of the beginning carver than the more experienced ones. If you don't have these particular sizes of gouges or tools, use something similar.

Each pattern in this book shows all the component pieces needed to make that particular carving. All the pieces are in a proportionate scale. If you desire larger or smaller versions, simply enlarge or shrink the chosen patterns on a photocopying machine. (In the "Tips" section, I explain reducing and enlarging patterns with a copying machine, if this is new to you.) You may also want to use the photocopying machine to make several sizes of the hand template. This way you will be sure to have a hand outline that is the proper size for the pattern you carve.

The numbers on the arms of some of the patterns correspond to numbers on the hand template, and are the suggested hands to use for that pattern. If you would rather use different hands, feel free to do so. This will allow you to achieve many different looks from just a few patterns. Each pattern also shows an assembled view of the pieces, so you can picture how the completed item might look if you desire to carve that pattern.

You will notice an arrow with a "G" superimposed on the patterns. This arrow indicates the recommended grain direction of the wood in relation to the pattern, in order to make carving that particular piece as easy as possible.

I use basswood whenever possible, but any softwood such as jelutong, clear spruce, or sugar/white pine will work equally well. If possible, use a bandsaw with a 1/8- or 3/16" blade to cut out the pattern pieces. The bandsaw will allow you to release the rough version of the pattern from the block of wood faster than a coping saw or other means.

General Notes

1. Trace the pattern pieces or make a copy of them on a photocopying machine. Glue the pattern you copied or traced onto some heavy paper such as poster paper or a manila file folder. When the glue is dry, cut out the pattern. This method will prevent you from ruining the master patterns in your book.

2. Lay your pattern on the wood, trace the outline of it, and saw it out. Pay close attention to any recommended grain directions indicated on the pattern pieces!!

3. You should now have a rough blank ready to be carved.

4. Use your own techniques and style to bring the carving to the finished stage.

5. You will notice that some of the patterns do not show hands attached to some of the arms. (This is where you will put the hand template to work). Many times the type of hands will be determined by what accessories you are going to include with the carving. Because you are carving the hands separately from the body, you can orient them to take advantage of the wood grain when you saw them out. This will allow you endless variations of hand positions, so you can give more life to your carvings. Also, if you are creating an extreme caricature, you can use a larger-than-normal hand pattern to add more humor to the carving. There is information in the "Tips" section describing hand carving separately from the arm, if you are not familiar with this technique.

6. I recommend that you read the entire book before starting the project. This will help you see where we are going, and will help alert you to carving techniques that may be unfamiliar. In the section where we paint the project, you may see an area or detail that might not have been clear to you in the carving section. Reading the entire book first will help you identify such areas and may help eliminate frustration at a later time. Remember, if we carve it we will paint it, so you will see everything at least twice.

7. If you see a pattern that you wish to carve, pay close attention to the pattern page. Although I submit all the patterns to the publisher full-size, it may be necessary for a certain number of them to be reduced in size in order to meet the page requirements of the book. If a particular pattern has been reduced in size, it will be indicated somewhere on the pattern. The information I included in the "Tips" section concerning enlarging/reducing will tell you how to get the pattern back to full-size, or any other size you may wish to make it.

Carving Tools

1/8" V gouge
1/4" V gouge
1/4" #8 U gouge
Fixed blade (Bütz) carving and detail knives—General wood removal and details such as eye carving.

For those of you who are not familiar with the type of cuts different gouges make, or how large the cut is for a specific size of gouge, I have included a Gouge Reference Chart in this book. If you want to use a different gouge other than one which I used, this chart will be helpful in determining what type of gouge you might want to try.

General Tips

1. Eyes

A. QUILT PIN METHOD: I often use various sizes of plastic-head quilting pins to make eyes. Mark where you want the eyes to be on the finished carving. Using a drill with a bit that is slightly larger than the pin head you are going to use, make a hole for each eye.

Using wire cutters, snip off the pin head, leaving about 1/4" of the pin attached to the head.

Insert the pin head into the eye socket, with the pin end going in first. Use a nail set to seat the head into the hole until only a small orb protrudes. This gives a fairly realistic eye without causing too much effort on your part. For extra detail, remove a triangular-shaped piece of wood from the sides of the pin head. This will make a very realistic eye when it is painted.

B. PUNCH METHOD: A second easy way to create eyes is to use carvers' eye punches. Select the size eye punch you want to use, based on the size of the eye sockets you have made. Push the eye punch against the socket firmly and rotate it. After making both eyes, remove triangular-shaped pieces of wood from the corners to give more detail. Use your knife, if necessary, to smooth and round off the eyeball.

C. FOOTBALL METHOD: A more realistic way to make eyes is to first carve the eye sockets so that about a 90-degree angle is formed. Lightly sketch in a football-shaped eye in each socket, such that the top half of the football is on the upper half of the socket, and the lower half of the football is on the lower half of the socket. When you sketch in the footballs, make the outside ends lower than the inside ends. Using the tip of your knife, score the football outline to a depth of about 1/16". Now use the tip of your knife to remove triangular-shaped pieces of wood from the left and right corner of each eye. This will leave a small section of wood inside each football, which will be the eyeball. Use your knife to round off and smooth the eyeball. You can vary the way you remove the triangular-shaped corners, if you want the eyes to be looking more to one side, rather than straight ahead.

D. MOUND METHOD: The most realistic way to make eyes is to first rough carve the nose so it is standing out from the face. Next, sketch a circle or oval on each side of the nose to represent where the eye mounds will be located. Using a smaller "V" gouge such as a 1/8" size, or your knife tip, go around the circles or ovals so the mounds will be defined, and separated from the face area. Use your knife to round the sharp edges of the mounds, and the face area around the mounds.

Divide the mounds into thirds by sketching two curved horizontal lines across each one, making sure that the lines join at each corner of the mound.(Look at your own eyes in a mirror to see what I mean here). Using your knife tip, score each horizontal line about 1/16" deep. Working from the *center* of the eye mound, use your knife tip to shave upward toward the top horizontal line and downward toward the bottom horizontal line. This will make the eyelids stand out from the eyeball area. Finally, remove small triangular pieces of wood from each corner of the eye, so the eyeball will be rounded from left to right, as well as top to bottom.

Changing the size and shape of the mounds and the spacing between the horizontal lines will allow you to achieve many effects and expressions on your carvings.

One last thing concerning eyes: Don't get upset if you discover that you have carved one eye smaller or at a different angle than the other eye. This "accident" may work to your advantage. It will lend an interesting variation to the carving, and no one has to know you didn't do it that way on purpose!!

2. Buying Wood

When buying wood, whether it be basswood, spruce, or some other type, try to pick the lightest pieces. They tend to have less fat and sap in them, so they are easier to carve.

3. Wrinkles and Folds

An easy way to help determine where you want to place wrinkles and folds in the arms, torso, and legs is to observe and note where the wood grain changes direction as you carve. Usually in the crook of an elbow or behind the knees, you will notice that wood "fuzzies" try to appear, no matter how carefully you carve or how sharp your knife is. That is because the wood grain direction is changing and you are trying to carve against the grain, thus the "fuzzies." These spots are perfect candidates for wrinkles and folds, which are made with a large "V" tool or by cutting wedges out with your knife. As a beginning carver, if you do nothing more than add a few cuts in these areas, you will be amazed at the difference in the way the carving looks. With experience, you will start noticing other places to add wrinkles and folds.

4. Enlarging and Reducing Patterns

For those of you who haven't had much practice enlarging or reducing patterns, or being able to calculate how much enlargement or reduction you need to select on the photocopying machine, here are some general guidelines:

Let's say you have a pattern that shows a side profile requiring 2"-thick wood and you want to make the pattern larger so it will fit on 3"-thick wood. Use the following formula to calculate what percentage enlargement to select on the copier:

[New Dimension Desired ÷ Present Dimension]
x 100 =
percent to select on copier machine.

Using our example, this would work out as follows:

[3" ÷ 2"] x 100 = 150 percent

Going the other way, let's say you have a pattern that shows a 2" side profile, and you want to reduce it to fit on a piece of 1-3/4"-thick wood. Using the same formula, it works out as follows:

[1.75" ÷ 2"] x 100 = 87.5 percent

If the machine you are using can't be set large enough or small enough to get the job done on the first try, additional steps may be required. Go ahead and make your first copy using the largest enlargement or reduction setting you can select. Measure the new dimensions on your copy, which will now be your present dimension, then use the same formula as before to calculate how much additional enlargement or reduction is needed to get the pattern to the size you desired it to be.

5. Holding Hands

When making separate hands that will hold some object, it is easiest if you first cut out the top profile of the hand, drill a hole large enough for the object to fit through, then saw out the side profile of the hand. This procedure will help prevent the hand from splitting when you drill it.

6. Basic Hands

For those patterns where the hands are to be carved separately, the following instructions may be used if you are not familiar with this method of hand carving:

(A) Lay out the top view of the hands on a piece of 3/4"-thick basswood. Leave a short section of wood at the rear of each hand when you lay out the pattern. This section will serve as a handle while you carve and shape the hands, and will form the wrist pegs in a later step. Saw out the top profile of the hands.

(B) Now, using the top set of hands in the Hand Studies as a reference, sketch in the side profile of the hands, then saw them out. You now should have two hands that will require very little work to finish.

(C) Sketch in the thumbs. Remove wood from each hand using a knife or a #7 10mm "U" gouge so that the thumbs are well-defined, then round off the sharp edges of the thumbs.

(D) Draw a line in the middle of the finger section to divide it in half. Now draw lines to divide each of these sections in half. You should now have four fingers defined, all approximately equal.

(E) Using a 1/8" "V" gouge, go over these lines so the fingers will be separated. *As an option*, to add further detail without too much pain on your part, use a bandsaw, scroll saw, or coping saw to carefully saw along these lines. Use your knife to remove any fuzzy wood caused by the saw cuts and to remove any sharp edges still remaining on the hands. At this point, if you do nothing else, you will have two hands that will look perfectly good once they are painted. Experienced carvers may add more detailing as they desire, such as knuckles and wrinkles on the finger joints.

(F) Use your knife to trim down the sections of wood protruding from the rear of the hands, so as to form a "wrist" or "pin" that will fit snugly into the holes you drilled earlier in the arms. When done properly, the hand should appear to be coming out of the sleeve. This method allows you to turn the hands in various directions so your carvings will appear more lifelike.

7. Stars

An easy way to make stars is to take a stylus or toothpick and put a dot of white paint where you want the star to be. Starting inside the dot, while the paint is still wet, drag the tip of the stylus or toothpick toward the edge and out to make a line. Do this for all five points of the star. The bigger you make the dot of paint to begin with, and the further you drag each line outside of the dot, the bigger the star will be.

Special Tips for Santas

1. For realistic fur, I use a product made by DecoArt called "Snowtex." This is a white, grainy, acrylic mixture that you apply with a small flat brush. After it is dry and painted, it gives a very good fur look.

2. If you don't want to try carving the "pompom" ball on Santa's hat, you can make one the easy way: Use unpainted wooden beads, which can be obtained at most craft stores. Buy various sizes, then use one which best fits the hat. After the head and hat are carved, create a flat spot on the hat and glue the bead to it. If the bead has a hole in it, fill the hole with wood filler after the glue dries.

An alternate choice is to drill a 1/8" hole into the hat, about 1/4" deep. Insert (glue) a short section of 1/8" wooden dowel into the hole. Put a small drop of glue on the end of the dowel and slide the bead onto the dowel until it is flush against the hat. When the glue is dry, use your knife to trim off any excess wood protruding from the bead. This method is the most realistic one I have found for making the pompoms.

Special Tips for Uncle Sams

1. I normally use the same thickness of wood for the head as I use for the body. This provides plenty of wood for a big floppy hat brim.

2. Saw out and carve the head separately from the main body. This gives you several advantages: (a) If you make a mistake on the head or body, the other part won't be ruined. (b) You can assemble the head to the body looking straight ahead, or you can turn it to one side.

Turning the head to one side will give more "life" to your carvings. (3) You can "mix and match" different heads with different bodies, therefore gaining more variations from a given number of patterns.

Special Tips for Leprechauns

1. An easy way to make gold "coins" for your leprechauns is to use various sizes of wooden dowels. Slice them thin with a band saw, coping saw, or other means, paint them gold, and place them as desired around the carving.

2. If you want to have pots of gold with your leprechaun, but don't want to try carving them, wooden candle cups make excellent pots. These are available at various craft and hobby stores and supply houses and come in many different sizes. Fill the bottom part with paper, paint the whole thing black, then put some of your wooden coins in the top part. You can make a realistic pot of gold quickly using this method. A scrap piece of wire makes an excellent handle for the pots.

3. If you want to make a wooden bench for your little guy to sit on, dowels also work well here. For example, you can cut a section of 3/4"-diameter dowel long enough to serve as the main bench part. Saw it in half lengthwise so you will have two half-round bench tops. Drill four 1/8" holes in the round side and insert four 1/8" dowel pieces in the holes to serve as legs. Cut them to the required length so the bench will just fit under your leprechaun. Stain the bench a nice wood color such as walnut. The more advanced carver may want to use various sizes of sticks and twigs to make a "real" leprechaun bench.

4. To make fishing poles and walking sticks, use small diameter wooden dowels, or scout around in your yard for small twigs and sticks if you want a more "authentic" look. Strong thread, such as quilting thread, makes excellent fishing line.

5. When drilling a hole in the body for the neck and head, you may wish to do so before you saw the body from the wood. First, transfer the side and front pattern profiles to the wood. Next, locate the center of the body on both profiles. Mark this location and drill down into the wood. Use a drill bit that is the proper size for the neck you carved and go deep enough into the block so you will have a neck hole after the body is sawed loose from the block. This method prevents the wood from splitting as you drill, especially in instances where you have a slim body profile.

Special Tips for Angels

1. For making the major pattern pieces, the following recommendations are given. If you wish to use different wood dimensions regarding thickness, by all means feel free to do so:

BODY: 1-3/4"- or 2"-thick basswood
ARMS: 3/4"-thick basswood
WINGS and FLOWING RIBBON: 1/16"- or 1/8"-thick hobby plywood (should be available at hobby or craft stores in your area)
HEARTS, etc.: basswood of sufficient thickness to accommodate the pattern piece. This will vary, depending on which pattern you are carving.
WOODEN DOWEL: 5/16" diameter, used to connect the angel to the mounting base.
SECTION OF 2" x 4" SCRAP WOOD: used as the base for the angel.

Special Tips for Snowmen

1. Use short sections of wooden dowels for the noses. Drill a hole in the snowman's face which will accommodate the dowel. Insert the dowel and trim it off so a short section protrudes from the face. Use your knife to trim it to a point so it looks like a carrot.

2. You may make the eyes, buttons, and mouth using hole punches of the proper diameter, or for more realism, use quilt pins with black heads. Trim off most of the pin, then insert the remainder into the face at the proper location. If you do this after the snowman is painted, it will prevent getting paint on the eyes and mouth.

3. Pipes are easily made using two small pieces of wooden dowel with slightly different diameters. Drill a hole in the snowman's mouth to accommodate the smaller of the two dowel sections. Insert the dowel and mark it so that a short section protrudes from the mouth.

Drill the proper size hole into the larger dowel and glue the smaller dowel into it. The larger dowel is the pipe bowl, and the smaller dowel is the pipe stem. Once the glue is dry, saw the pipe bowl to the proper size so your assembly looks like a pipe.

For a bit more realism, use your drill and carefully drill down a short distance into the top of the bowl so a hole is created. Paint the pipe and glue it into the mouth after painting the snowman.

General Painting Suggestions

I have included some suggested colors and paint brushes for all patterns. If you have a preference for a different color scheme, by all means use it. After all, it's your carving and you can paint it any way you desire.

I have also listed the colors produced by DecoArt and their identification numbers, which I have found to be suitable for painting these carvings. I have used these colors and the results were excellent. I hope this will help minimize your confusion when trying to sort through the maze of paint brands and colors at your hobby or craft store.

I have found that the best paintbrushes for the money are made by the Royal Brush Mfg. Inc. They come in a wide assortment of sizes and shapes, are durable, and, most importantly, are affordable. In general, here are the ones I use and recommend for painting your carvings:

> Royal Golden Taklon Series 250 Round, Size 0 and 00: Details such as eyes and other small areas.
>
> Royal Golden Taklon Series 170 Cat's Tongue, Size 2 and 4: Large areas.
>
> Royal Golden Taklon Series 150 Short Shader, Size 2 and 4: For blending colors, like blending a "blush" color into the flesh color on faces, hands, etc.

You may have heard and read this a million times, but when painting your carvings, keep the word **thin** in mind. What you want to do is stain the wood to give it some color and life, but you don't want the paint so thick that it covers up the beauty of the wood. *NOTE:* When painting faces and hair, I generally use a little thicker mixture of paint than I use on the rest of the carving. I want the face to be a bit more intense than the rest of the carving, since the head and face set the mood for the carving.

Suggested Colors

For Christmas (Santas)

Titanium White #DA1 (Hair, beards, eyes)
Buttermilk #DA3 (Fur)
Fleshtone #DA78 (Skin areas)
Blush Flesh #DA110 ("Windburning" effects)
Baby Blue #DA42 (Eyes)
Lamp Black #DA67 (Eyes, mittens)
Santa Red #DA170 (Robes, hats)
Burnt Umber #DA64 (Shoe and boot soles)
Red Iron Oxide #DA96 (Upper part of shoes, boots)
Oak Antiquing Gel #DS30 (Aging the finished carving)
Clear Satin Varnish #DS15 (Sealing the finished carving)
SnowTex (For making "fur" on hats and clothing)

For Valentine's Day (Angels)

Titanium White #DA1 (Eyes, highlight in eyes)
Buttermilk #DA3 (Wings)
Lamp (Ebony) Black #DA67 (Eye dots)
Fleshtone #DA78 (Face, hands, feet)
Baby Blue #DA42 (Eye dots)
Blush Flesh #DA110 (Blush on cheeks and around mouth)

Berry Red #DA19 (Ribbons, hearts)
Prussian Blue #DA138 (Ribbons)
Cadmium Yellow #DA10 (Hair and eyebrows)
Antique Gold #DA146 (Hair and eyebrows)
Sable Brown #DA61 (Hair and eyebrows)
Dark Chocolate #DA65 (Hair and eyebrows)
Lavender #DA34 (Robe)
Plum #DA175 (Robe)
Boysenberry Pink #DA29 (Robe)
Santa Red #DA170 (Robe)
Yellow Green #DA134 (Robe)
Williamsburg Blue #DA40 (Robe)
True Blue #DA36 (Robe)
Sapphire #DA99 (Robe)

For Fourth of July (Uncle Sam)

Titanium White #DA1 (Hair, eyebrows, eyes, stripes, stars)
Lamp Black #DA67 (Shoes, dot in eyes, buttons)
Fleshtone #DA78 (Face, hands)
Blush Flesh #DA110 (For blending on face and nose areas)
Baby Blue #DA42 (Light blue for dot in eyes)
Emperor's Gold #DA148 (Buttons on coat)
Calico Red #DA20 (Stripes)
Navy Blue #DA35 (Hat, coat, flags, firecrackers)
Antique Gold #DA9 (Vest)

For St. Patrick's Day (Leprechauns)

Titanium White #DA1 (Shirt, eyes)
Light Buttermilk #DA164 (Stockings)
Fleshtone #DA78 (All skin areas)
Blush Flesh #DA110 (Adding "blush" to nose and cheeks)
Burnt Sienna #DA63 (Upper part of shoes)
Burnt Umber #DA64 (Soles of shoes)
Tangerine #DA12 (Beard, hair, eyebrows)
Sable Brown #DA61 (Dot in eyes)
Milk Chocolate #DA174 (Trousers)
Viridian Green #DA108 (Hat, coat)
Kelly Green #DA55 (Shamrocks, stripes on stockings)
Emperor's Gold #DA148 (Buttons on coat, buckles on hat and shoes, coins)
Country Blue #DA41 (Stripes on stockings)

For Christmas (Snowmen)

Titanium White #DA1 (Main body of snowman)
Lamp Black #DA67 (Mittens, "coal" eyes and mouth, top hat, "coal" buttons on body)
Tangerine #DA12 ("Carrot" nose)
Burnt Umber #DA64 (Pipe and pipe stem)

For Halloween (Ghost, Witch, Pumpkin)

Titanium White #DA1 (Ghost, Witch's hair and eyes)
Tangerine #DA12 (Pumpkin)
Lamp Black #DA67 (Ghost eyes and mouth, Pumpkin eyes, nose and mouth, clothing on witch)
Burnt Sienna #DA63 (Pumpkin stem, witch's boots, broom handle)
Antique Gold #DA146 (Broom straw)
Fleshtone #DA78 (All skin areas)
Blush Flesh #DA110 (Blush on nose and cheeks)

For Thanksgiving (Pilgrims)

Fleshtone #DA78 (All skin areas)
Blush Flesh #DA110 (Blush for nose and cheek)
Titanium White #DA1 (Eyes, highlights in black dot of eye, trim on coat, trim on dress, woman's cap, woman's apron, man's stockings)
Baby Blue #DA42 (Large dot in eye)
Lamp Black #DA67 (Smaller dot in eye, man's hat, buttons on woman's apron)
Golden Straw #DA168 (Woman's hair and eyebrows)
Sable Brown #DA61 (Man's hair and eyebrows)
Raw Umber #DA130 (Rifle Stock)
Shimmering Silver #DA70 (Rifle barrel and trigger, buckle on hatband, buckle on shoes)
Neutral Grey #DA95 (Man's coat and pants, woman's dress)
Light Cinnamon #DA114 (Man's shoes, food bag)

Suggested colors for Easter (Rabbits)

Light Buttermilk #DA164 (Head and feet)
Titanium White #DA1 (Eyes, highlight in black dot of eye)
Baby Blue #DA42 (Large dot in eye)
Lamp Black #DA67 (Smaller dot in eye, nose)
Berry Red #DA19 (Shirt)
Country Blue #DA41 (Overalls, bow on head)
Shimmering Silver #DA70 (Buttons on overall straps, belt buckle)
Honey Brown #DA163 (Purse)
Burnt Sienna #DA63 (Belt)
Various colors of your choice: (Easter egg)

Remember: These are only a few of the many colors you can use for your carvings. Should you have other color preferences, use them. Don't be afraid to get wild and experiment with all sorts of color combinations. For those of you (like me) who have difficulty trying to decide which colors work well together, most hobby and art-supply stores sell inexpensive color wheels which will show you colors that work together and colors that oppose each other. I have listed a few combinations here, for illustrative purposes:

Main Color	Contrast Color
Red	Green
Orange	Blue
Yellow	Violet

A good color wheel will not only show you main and contrasting colors, it will also show colors that blend.

Carving the Project

For this project we are going to carve a Santa with a European or "old-world" type look. For beginners, this project should help you with details such as facial features, hands, and shoes. I wanted to keep it simple so you wouldn't go bankrupt trying to acquire the tools necessary to carve or paint it, yet give you a chance to work on various aspects of carving as we move through the different steps. Almost all of the carving is done with a bench and detail knife, and only a couple of gouges are needed. Only one block of wood is required, so you won't have to worry about carving a multitude of pieces and then trying to fit them together. I have kept the detailing of the project (such as texturing the beard and hair) to a minimum. You will discover that with some carvings, "less is really more," and in this case I wanted to keep the detailing within reach of beginners' abilities. You more experienced carvers should feel free to add as many extra details as desired.

In the carving steps, I will be referring to (and using), two different knives as we move through the steps. If I only mention the word "knife," I am referring to a typical fixed-blade bench carving knife. If I specify "detail knife," I am referring to a knife that has a slimmer blade and tip so you can cut in details that the wider-bladed bench knife may not allow you to do.

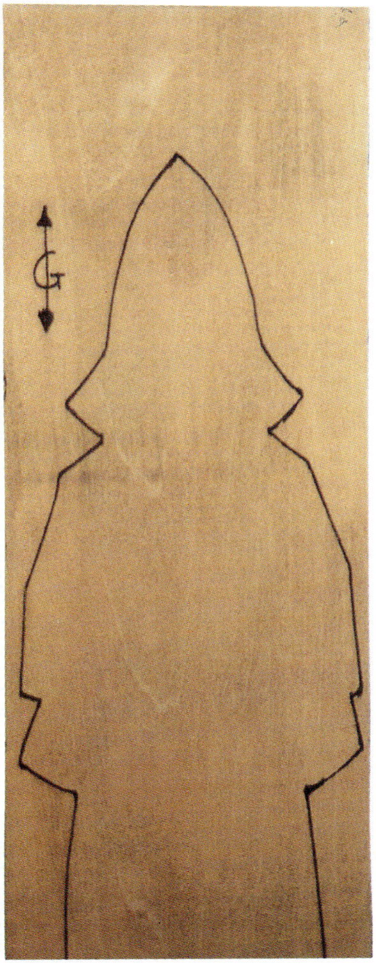

Transfer the front view of the pattern to an appropriately-sized piece of 1-3/4"-thick wood. Pay close attention to the indicated direction of the wood grain on the pattern. By having the grain run vertically through the head and body, your carving experience will be more pleasant and adding details to the carving later will be much easier.

Next, transfer the side view of the pattern to the wood.

Saw away excess wood from the left side of the pattern, but leave a few "tabs," as I have done here. These tabs will help hold the wood level when we saw out the side profile in a moment.

Make saw cuts on the right side of the body as shown here, but **do not** cut the wood completely away from the body at this time. (We need to keep the wood on this side of the body intact until we saw out the side profile)

Next, lay the wood flat again and saw away all the excess wood from the body, including the tabs. Now we are ready to begin some serious roughin' out of the arms and other features. Grab a cup of coffee or other refreshment and let's get busy!

Lay the wood on its edge and saw out the side profile completely. Here is where you will appreciate the tabs you left in place earlier.

Referring to the pattern, sketch a line down the right side of the body to define and separate the arm from the body, in front ...

... and in back.

Again referring to the pattern, sketch lines down the right side of the body to define the width of the right arm and hand. (This is slightly different than what the side view of the pattern shows, but remember that patterns are just guides to get you started, and references to look at as you move through the carving stages.) Then, using the tip of your knife, incise the lines approximately 1/8" deep in order to create some "stop cuts" which will help control our wood removal.

Here is how it looks after a few cuts.

We are going to remove the darkened sections of wood. You may use your knife, a flat gouge, or any other tool that works best for you. Work from the front of the body back to the arm, slicing away the wood. You will have to keep incising the lines and shaving away wood until the section is removed.

Here all the darkened wood has been removed in front. At this time, don't worry about the head and beard areas. We are going to work on them later. For now, let's concentrate on removing excess wood from the arms in order to give us better access to the rest of the body.

Now repeat this process for the section of darkened wood in back. At this point the right side of the body should look something like this.

Apply these same techniques to the other side to define and separate the left arm from the body.

And do the same thing on the sharp edge in the right rear.

Now that the four severe sharp edges have been removed, the body has taken on an octagonal shape, and we now have eight smaller sharp edges. Using your knife, shave away these eight sharp edges again at about a 45-degree angle (but on a smaller scale), and our body should be round enough to live with.

Use your knife to knock off the right front edge all the way up through the beard and head area, at about a 45 degree angle.

Repeat this process for the two sharp edges on the left side of the body.

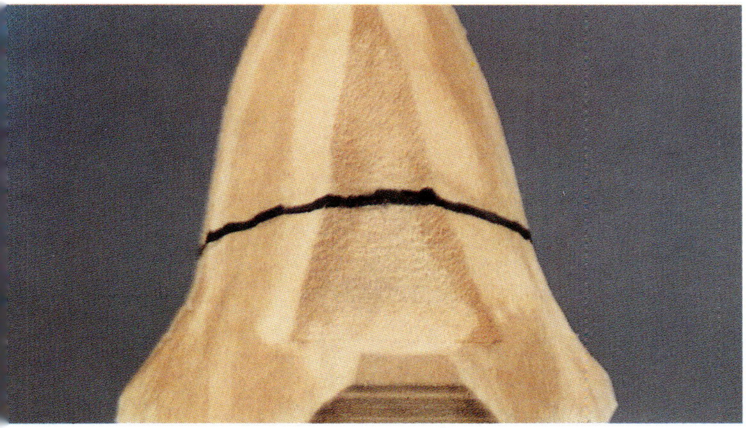

Sketch a line around the head to define the separation between the hat and hair, then incise this line about 1/8" deep with the tip of your knife.

Sketch a line as shown to indicate the separation between the hair and beard on the right side of the face. Incise this line about 1/8" deep with your knife.

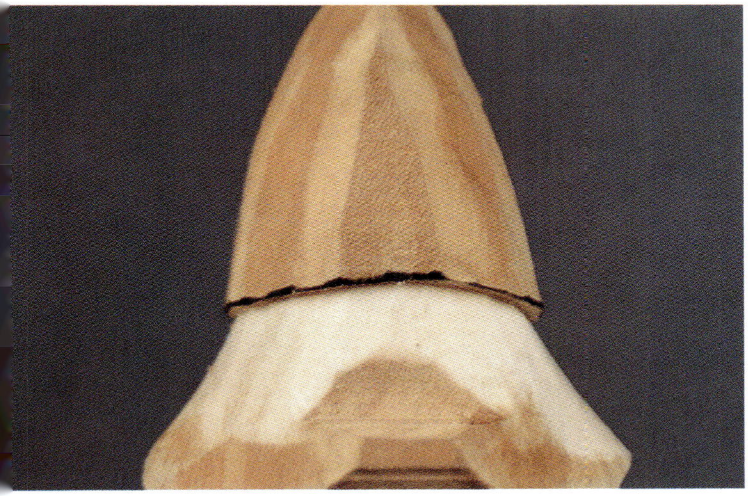

Working from the bottom of the head, use your knife to shave up toward the line you just incised, all the way around the head. This will make the face and hair appear as if they are going into the hat, and also gets our detailing process started.

Now, use your knife to shave away the darkened section of wood.

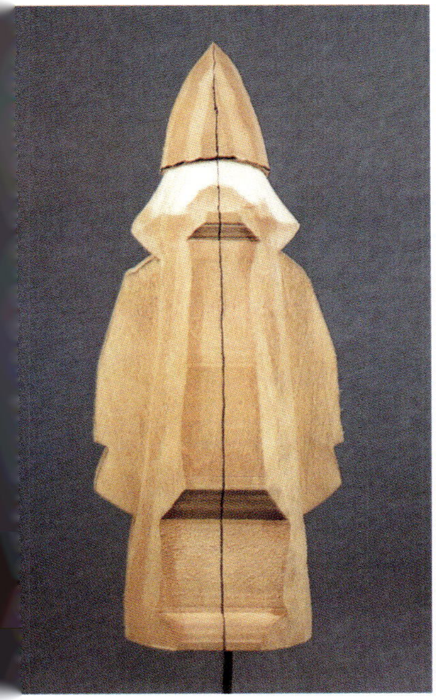

At this time, to help maintain symmetry as we carve the face and other details, sketch a line all the way down the front and back of the body to indicate the approximate centerline.

Keep removing wood in this area until the beard and face are at the same level, as shown here.

Next, use your knife to clip off the lower front edge of the hair at about a 45-degree angle.

Clip off the rear bottom edge of the hair at about a 45-degree angle, also.

Now repeat these preliminary steps on the left side of the face and hair.

Before going any further with the face, let's finish the arms and hands so we'll have a better idea about where we want the beard line to be placed. First, use your knife to knock off the two sharp edges of the right arm at about a 45-degree angle. (Are you starting to see a pattern developing here)?

Now, use your knife to remove the new sharp edges you just created.

Sketch a line to define the separation of the hand and sleeve, then incise this line about 1/8" deep with the tip of your knife.

Working from the bottom of the hand, shave up *toward* the sleeve to remove a layer of wood and make the hand appear as if it is going up into the sleeve.

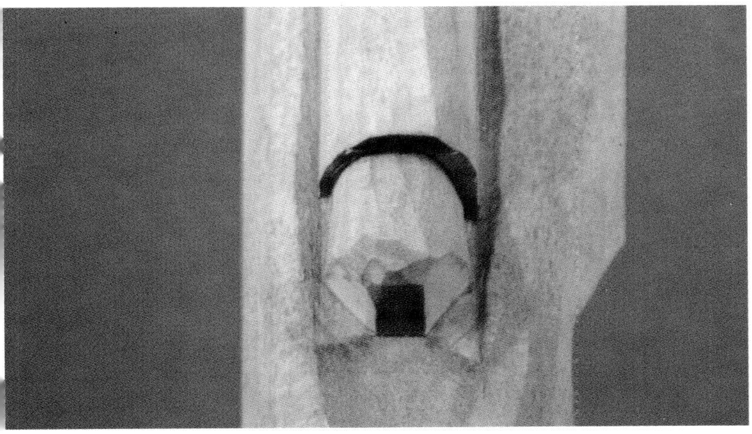

Next, clip off the front and rear edges of the hand at about a 45-degree angle.

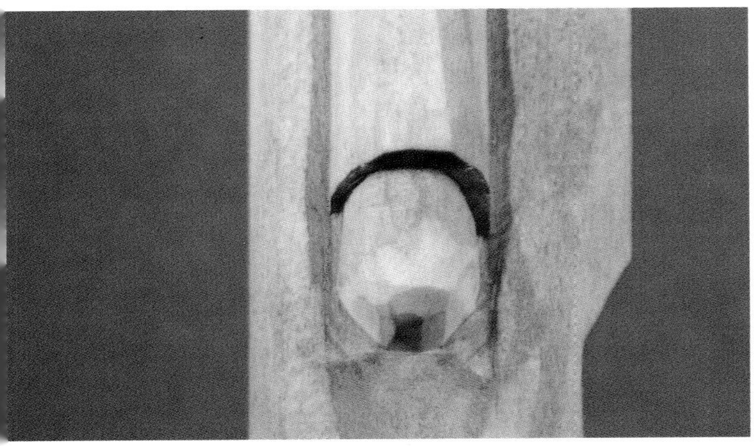

Use your knife to remove any remaining sharp edges on the hand.

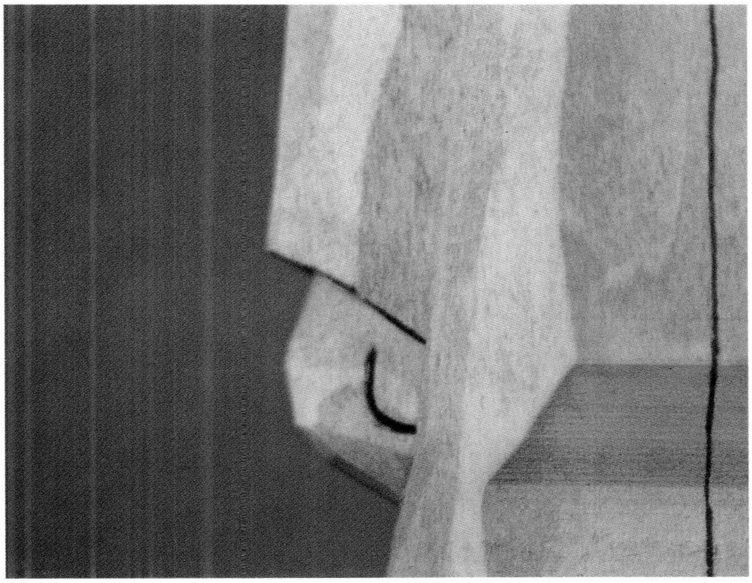

Sketch a line to indicate the separation of the thumb and fingers, and incise the line about 1/8" deep with your knife tip.

Using your knife tip, shave *downward* on the finger portion of the hand. This will remove a small amount of wood, causing the thumb to stand out from the finger portion of the hand. Then lightly shave the sharp edge from the thumb so it will be slightly rounded off.

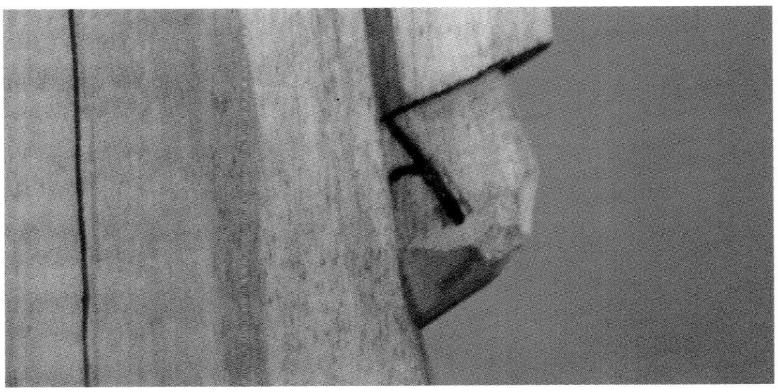

Sketch the finger (mitten) curl lines on the rear of the hand, and incise them about 1/8" deep with your knife tip.

Now remove wood from this area, following the lines you incised. To do this, use the tip of your knife and cut at about a 45-degree angle, so small "V" channels are formed when the wood comes away. Look over this arm and hand, and if there are any areas that have been untouched by your knife, lightly shave away wood from these areas. This will "surface" the entire arm and hand, removing any saw marks and making the wood more receptive to painting later.

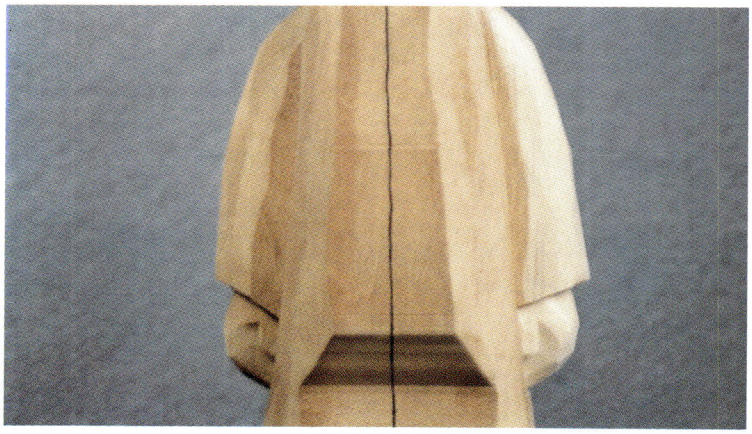

Repeat this entire process on the left arm to bring it to a finished state.

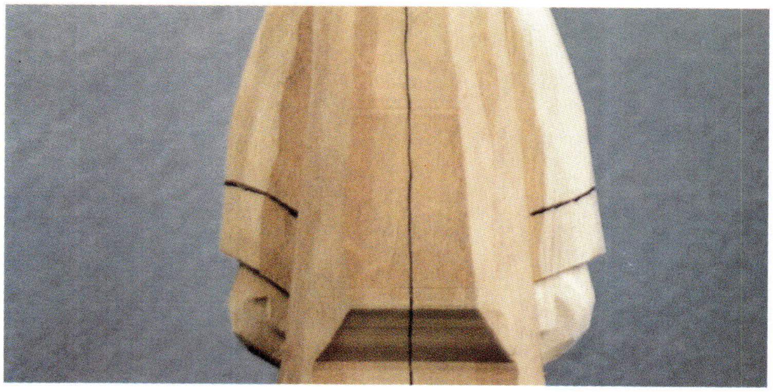

Sketch the fur lines on the sleeves and incise the lines about 1/8" deep with your knife.

Shave *down* slightly from above the fur, *toward* the lines you incised. This will remove a small amount of wood, causing the fur sections to stand out from the sleeves.

The back of the robe around the neck area still needs a little refining, so let's take care of that now. Using your knife and working *upward*, shave away some of the wood so the robe flows smoothly up to the bottom of the hair.

Now, use your knife to shave away all the sharp edges from the hair, all the way around. Repeat as necessary until no severe sharp edges remain on the hair section.

Since I know you can't stand the suspense any longer, let's get serious about putting a face on this guy. First, sketch some lines to define the width of the nose. Leave the nose a little wider than you think it should be for now. You can always slim it down later if it looks too big, but it's real difficult to make it wider once the wood is gone! Then, incise these lines with your knife, about 1/8" deep.

We want to remove the darkened sections of wood with a knife or flat gouge in order to make the nose stand out from the face.

Keep incising and shaving away wood as necessary until you get the darkened sections removed, similar to what you see in this front view...

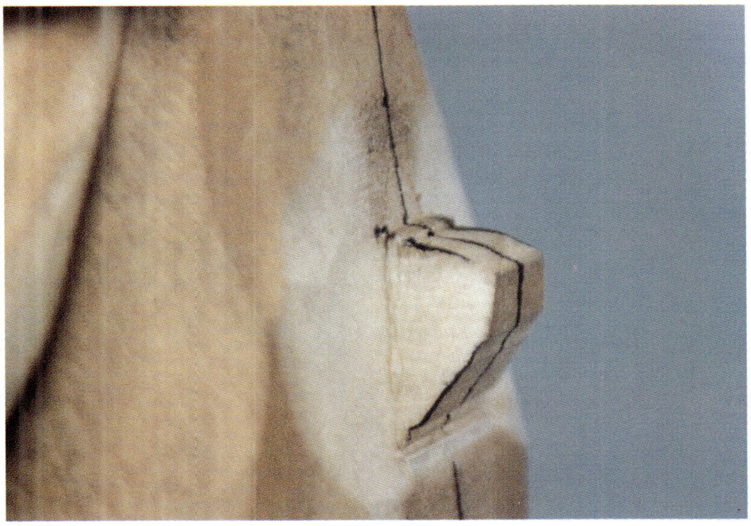

... and from a side angle.

Now clip off the *lower* corners of the nose at about a 45-degree angle.

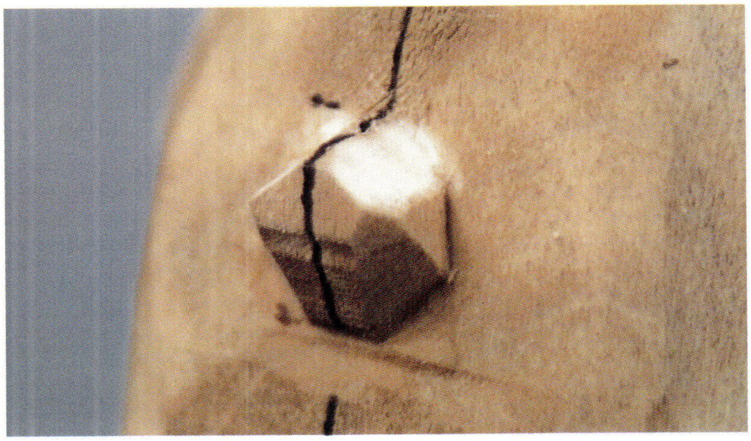

Then do the same thing on the top corners of the nose.

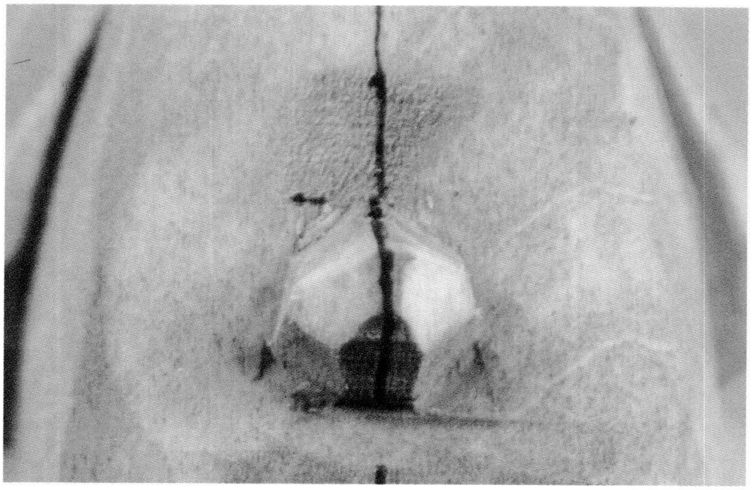

Next, clip off the two sharp edges on the front of the nose at about a 45-degree angle.

Now, shave away all the remaining severe sharp edges on the nose, and the nose should be fairly round.

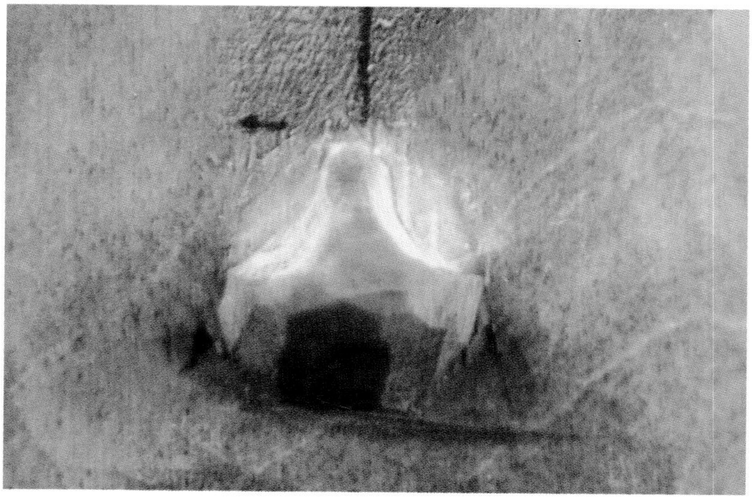

To create a nostril flare, scoop *in and up* on both sides of the nose, using the tip of your knife.

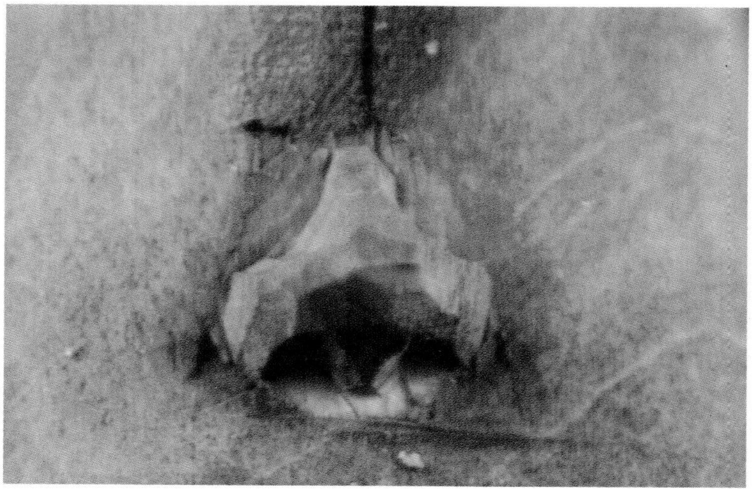

Use your detail knife tip to remove two "V"-shaped chips of wood from the bottom of the nose to simulate nostril openings.

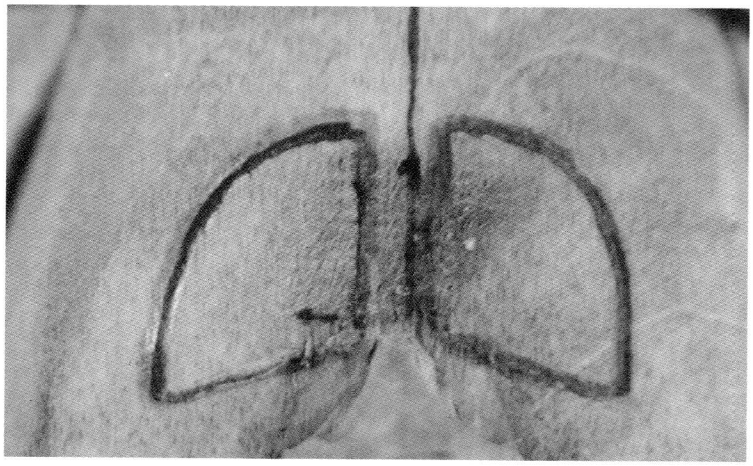

Now, to start the eyes, sketch some lines as shown. Incise these lines about 1/8" deep with your detail knife.

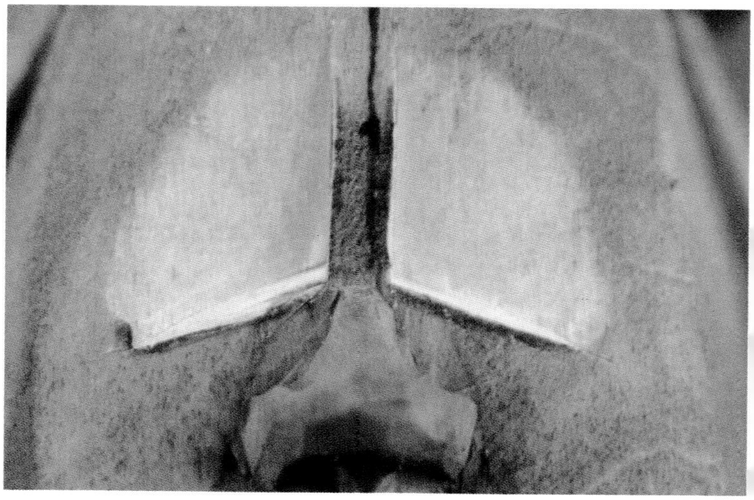

Shave *in and up* with your detail knife, working from the outer edges of the face in toward the nose, to form the eye areas as shown in this front view...

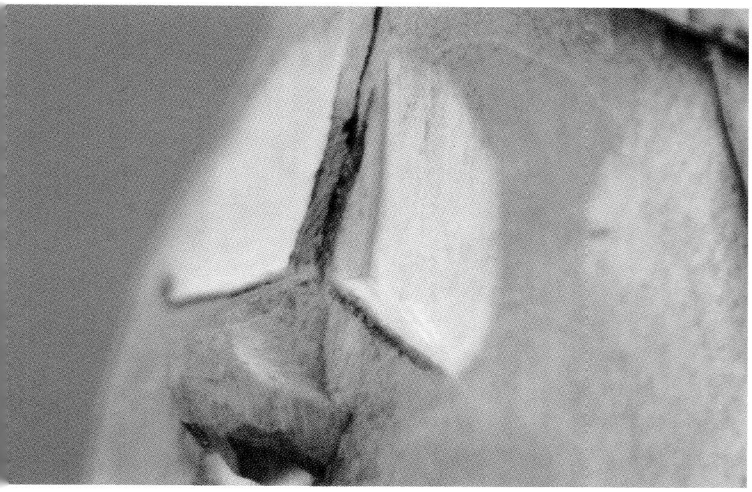

... and in this angle view.

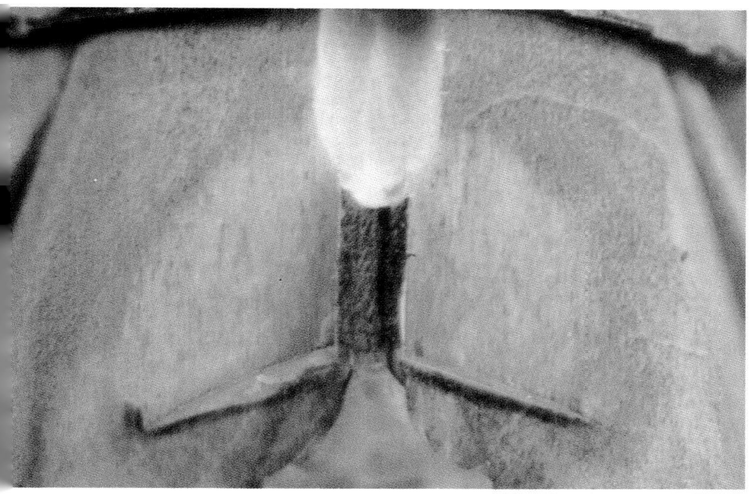

Using a 1/4" No. 8 "U" gouge, remove a section of wood at the top of the nose to separate the eyes and form the division between the eyebrows.

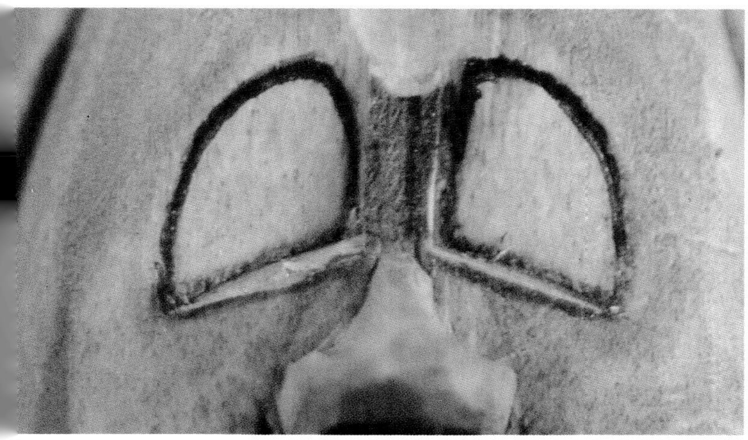

Now, sketch in two eyes as shown, and incise the lines all the way around about 1/8" deep with the tip of your detail knife. These big eyes will give the little guy a real friendly look when painted, and they are fun to carve.

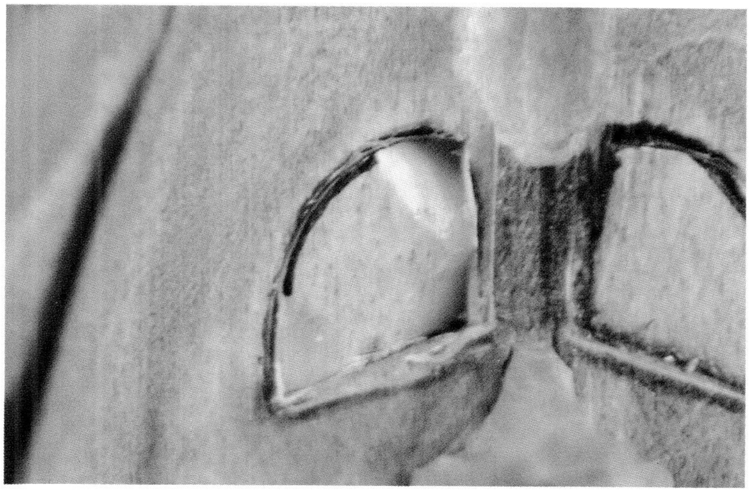

Using the tip of your detail knife, clip the two inside corners and the lower outside corner of the right eye at about a 45-degree angle and remove the small chips of wood.

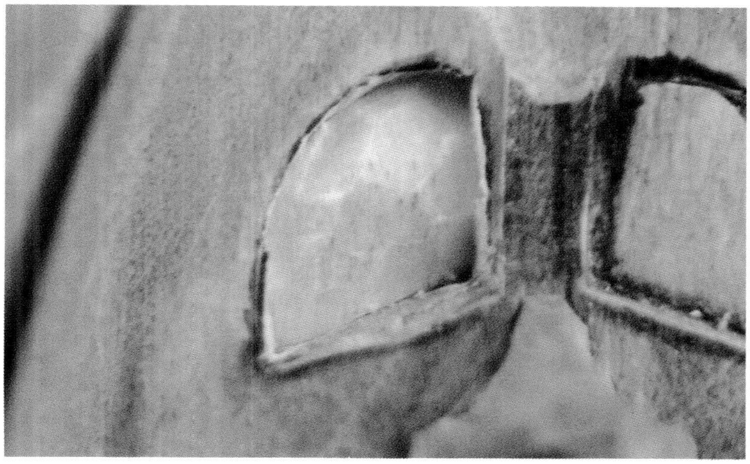

Now use your detail knife to remove the remaining edges of the eye at about the same angle. Then round off any sharp edges that may still be there, and the eye is done.

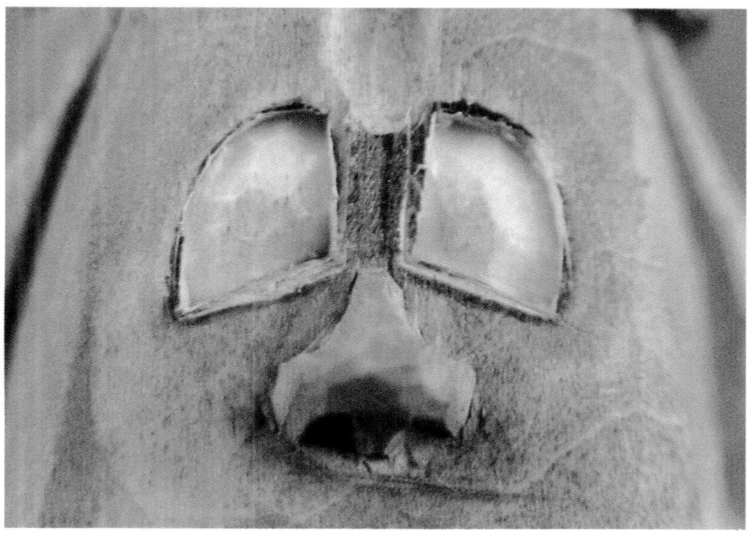

Repeat this process for the other eye.

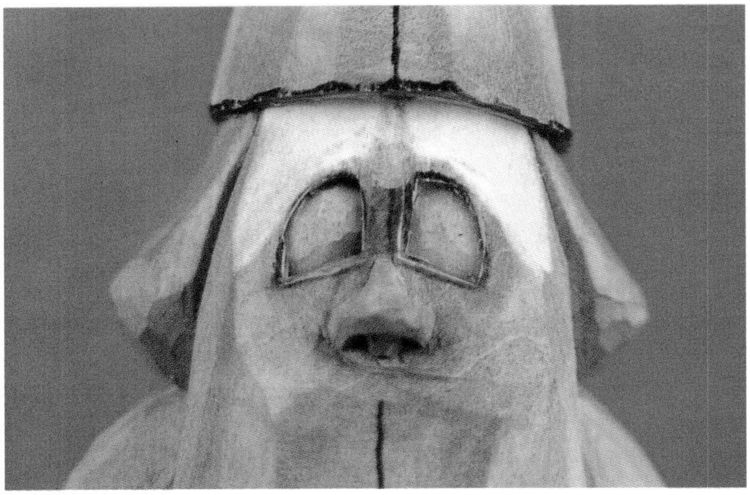

To form the eyebrows, use your detail knife and with an upward scooping motion, remove a small amount of wood above and along the sides of the eyes.

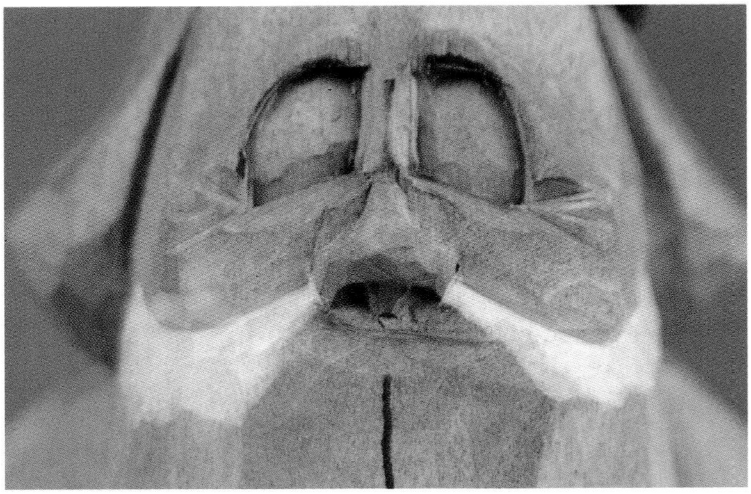

Using your knife shave *down* toward the line, and shave *up* toward the line, so a "V"-shaped channel is formed to separate the cheeks from the beard and mustache.

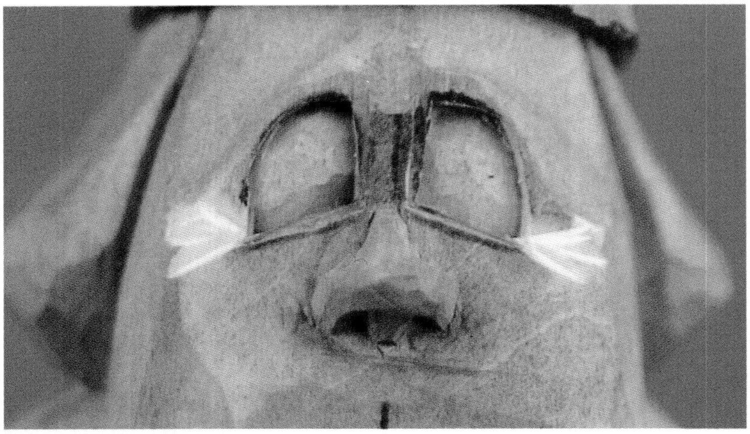

Last, let's put a few wrinkles in the corner of each eye to add a bit more character to our little fella. With your knife or 1/8" "V" gouge, cut a few "V"-shaped wrinkles into the face.

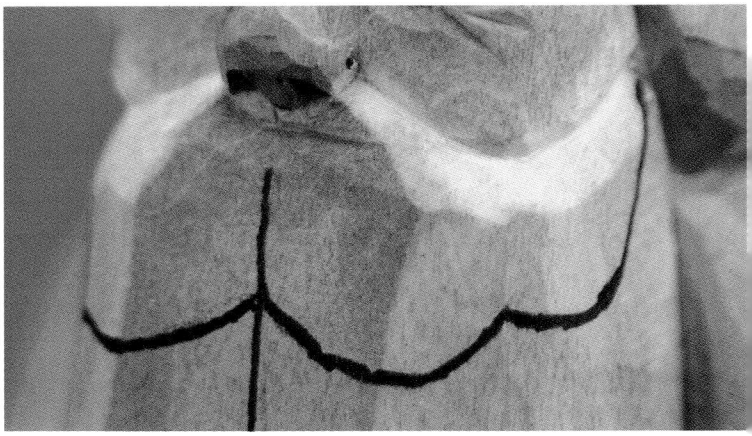

We are going to put a happy little mustache on this guy, so sketch in some lines as shown. Then, incise the lines about 1/8" deep with your knife.

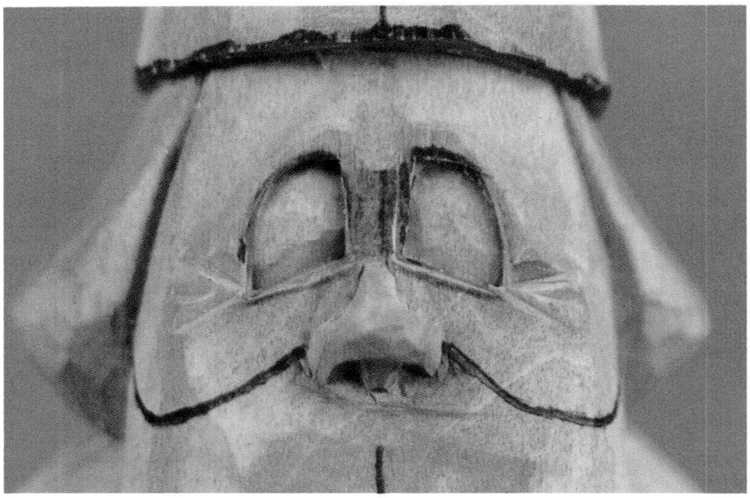

Sketch in the cheek lines, and incise them about 1/8" deep with your detail knife tip.

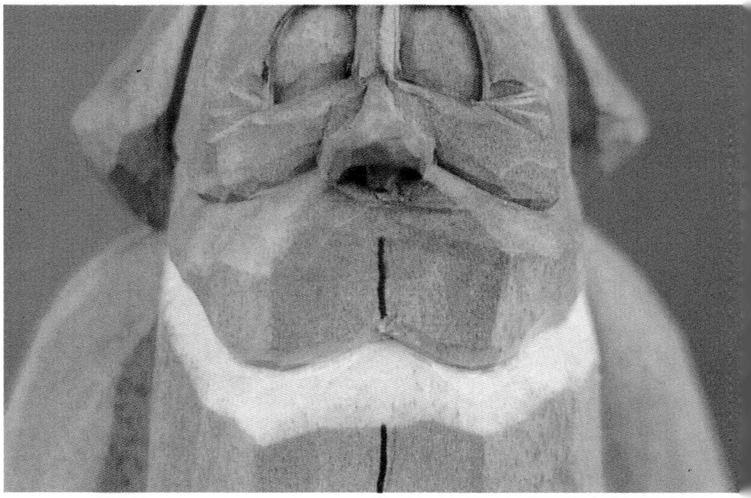

Shave *down* toward the lines and *up* toward the lines you just incised to make the mustache stand out.

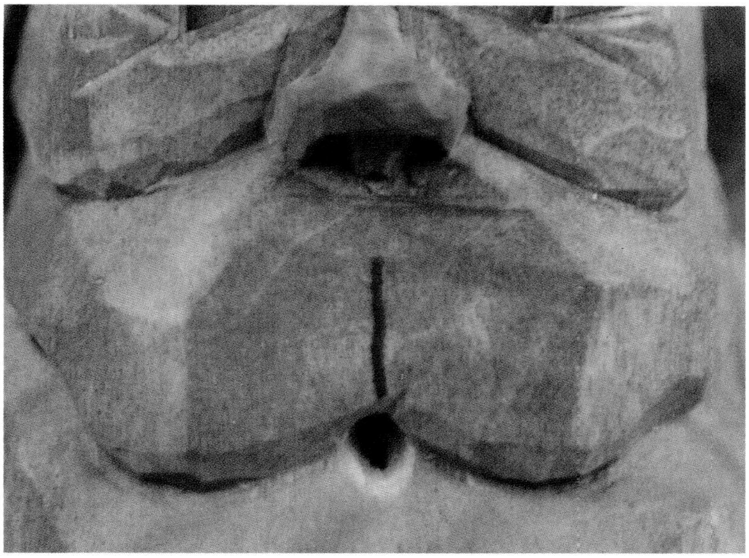

To form a mouth, use a 1/8" nail punch or a drill with a 1/8" bit and make a hole in the face as shown.

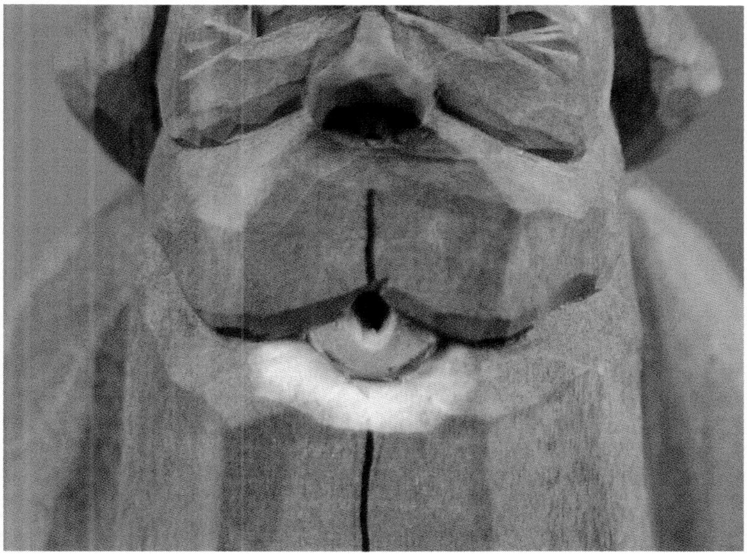

Clip off the sharp point at the bottom of the lip section and round off any remaining sharp corners.

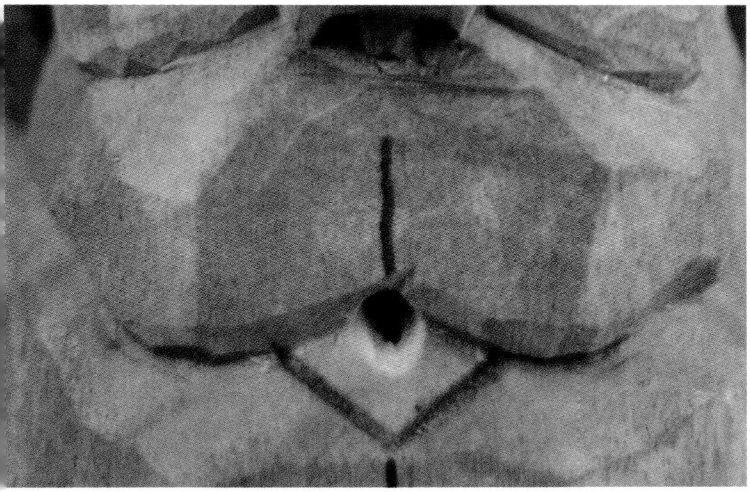

The bottom lip is made by first sketching some lines and incising them lightly with your detail knife.

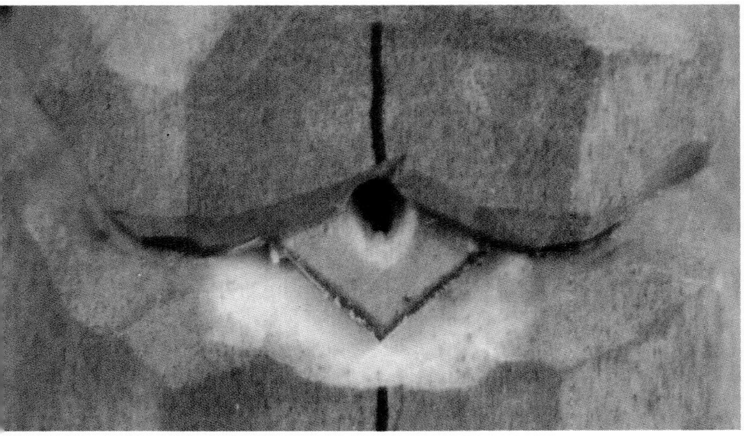

Shave *up* toward the lines to remove a small amount of wood and make the lip section stand out.

Referring to the pattern, sketch a line to define the bottom of the beard, then incise it with your knife as we have been doing on other steps.

As before, shave toward the incision from both directions in order to make the beard stand out from the robe.

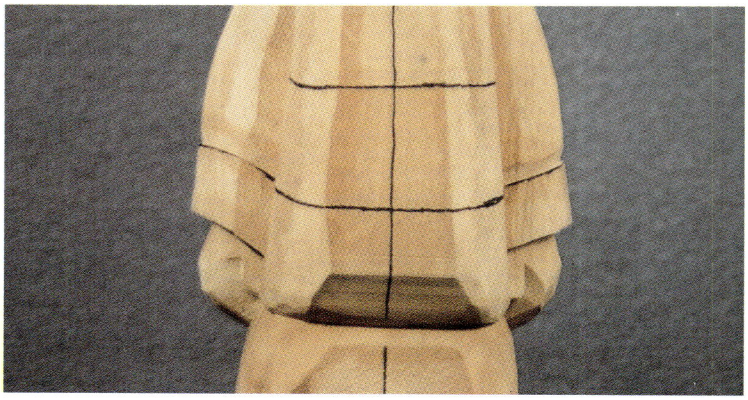

Now, since I want to give this guy a slightly European-style beard, the first thing I want to do is sketch two more lines on the beard and incise them.

Shave *down* toward the lines, and also shave *up* toward the lines. As you shave up, remove the greatest amount of wood at the top of each section, so the beard sections will acquire the layered look as depicted on the pattern.

Here is a side view to help show these layered sections.

To add some texture to the hair and beard yet maintain the "bold" carving look, I have used a 1/4" #8 "U" gouge to cut in some detail on the beard. (I will repeat this procedure on the hair before we paint the project.)

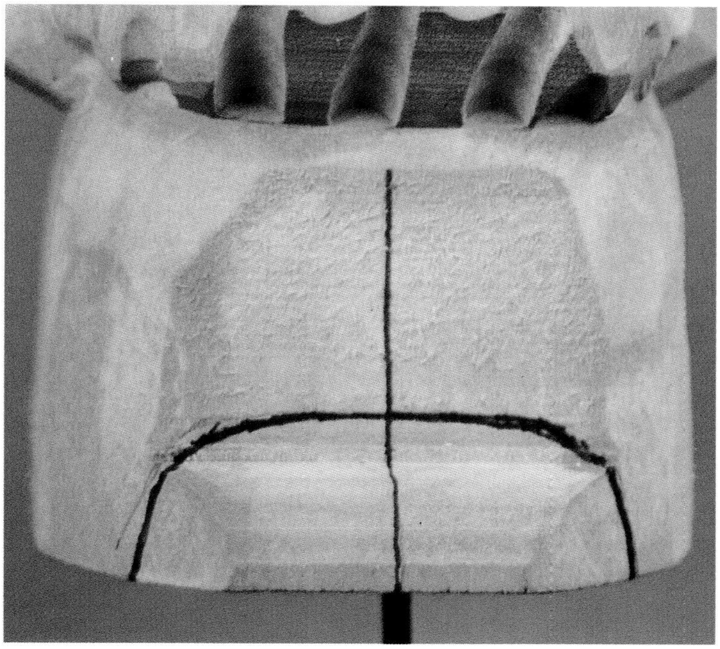

Okay, now that we've got the hard work out of the way, let's give this rascal some shoes, finish off a few minor things, and then we can move on to the painting. First, sketch lines as indicated to establish the shoe width and incise them with your knife.

... and here it is from the side.

Remove the darkened sections of wood to make the shoes stand out from the robe, and also to form the separation between the shoes.

Next, round off the toes and upper part of the shoes using your knife.

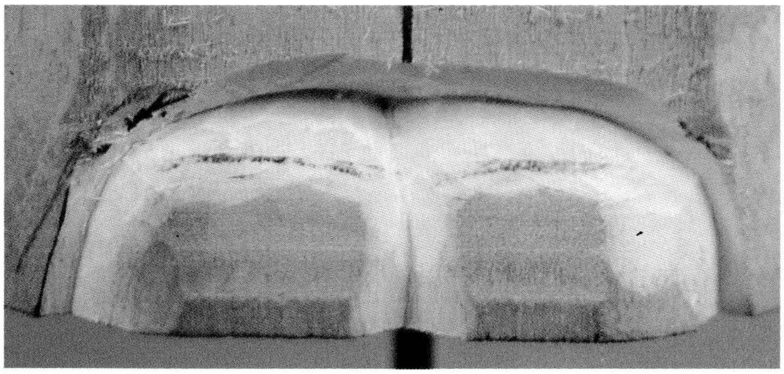

Here's a front view ...

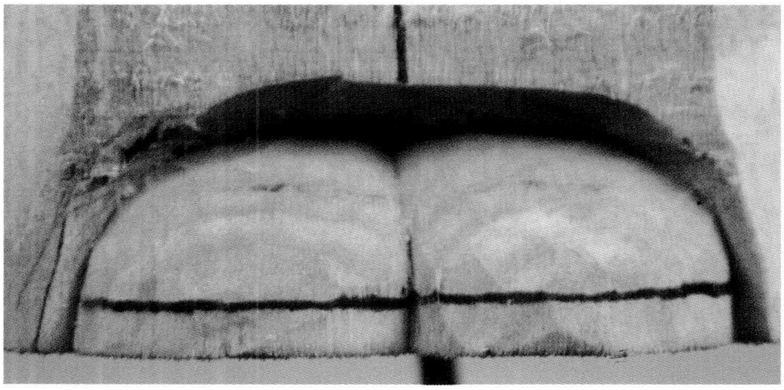

To create the soles of the shoes , sketch a line as shown, then *lightly* incise this line with your knife tip.

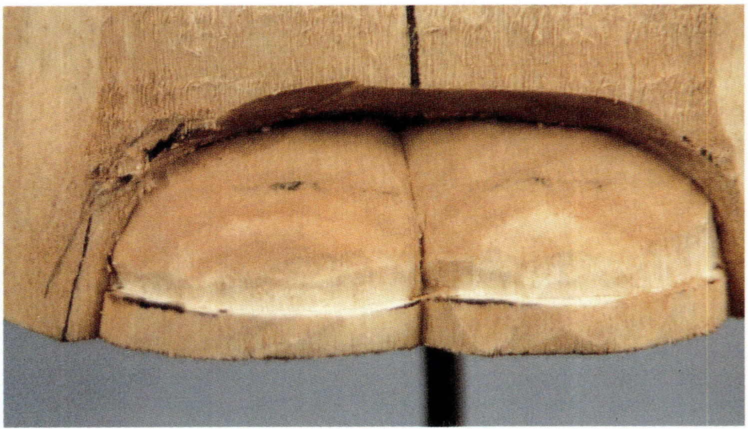

Now, working from the *top* part of the shoes, very carefully and lightly shave *down toward* the incision. This will remove a small amount of wood from the upper shoe, and will make the soles stand out.

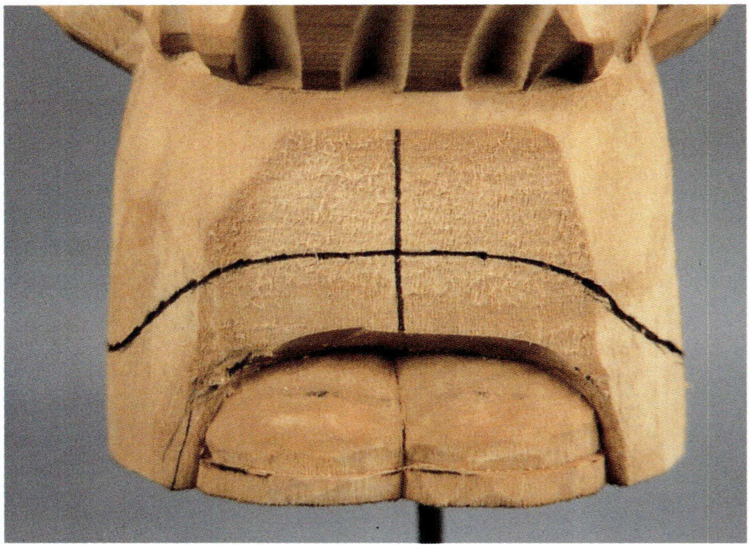

Referring to the pattern, sketch a line to indicate the location of the fur around the bottom of the robe.

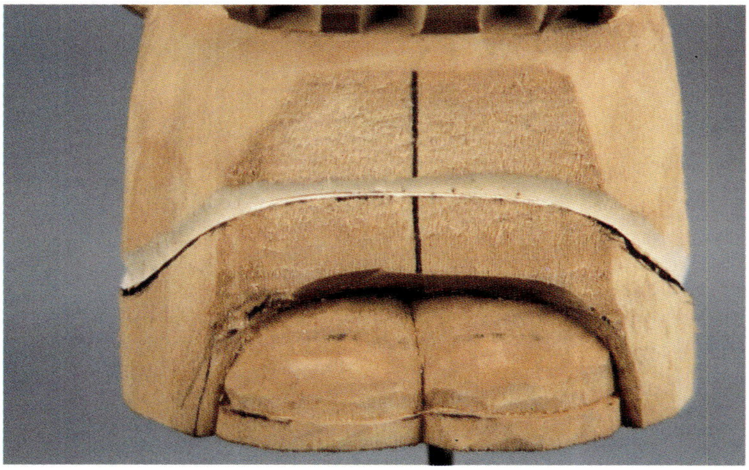

Bring this fur detail to life in the same manner as you did on the sleeves.

Now, just to add a little extra detail to the fur on the sleeves and robe, I have used an 8mm #7 "U" gouge to remove random sections of wood to create a textured effect. At this point, we are through with the basic carving process. I am going to add one other detail, a pompom on the hat, as an option just to show you an easy way to do it. Look over your carving and if you see any areas that have not been visited by a knife or gouge, go ahead and surface these areas now so the wood will be ready to receive some paint and start coming to life.

Optional Pompom steps

Although there is no pompom or fur shown on the hat on the pattern, I am going to include them here just to give you a little something extra for your money. It is your option as to whether or not you want to add this to your carving, and the carving will look just fine if you decide to omit these steps. As I described in the "Tips" section, here is the easy way to make a pompom. First decide where on the hat you want the pompom to be located. I am going to put one on the right side of this hat, so I marked with a dot where I wanted to drill a 1/8"-diameter hole, about 1/4" deep.

Once the hole is drilled, sketch the pompom flap lines down from the top of the hat, as shown.

Go over these lines with a 1/8" "V" gouge to define them.

Using your knife, shave away a small amount of wood from the hat on both sides of the flap so it will be better defined and will stand out from the hat. Also, lightly shave away any sharp edges on the flap at this time.

Now, sketch a fur line around the entire hat as shown here. Since the flap is "hanging down" over the fur, do not sketch fur in the flap area.

As you did on the sleeves and robe, remove a small amount of wood so the fur will be defined. If desired, you may also use your gouge to add texture to this fur, as I did.

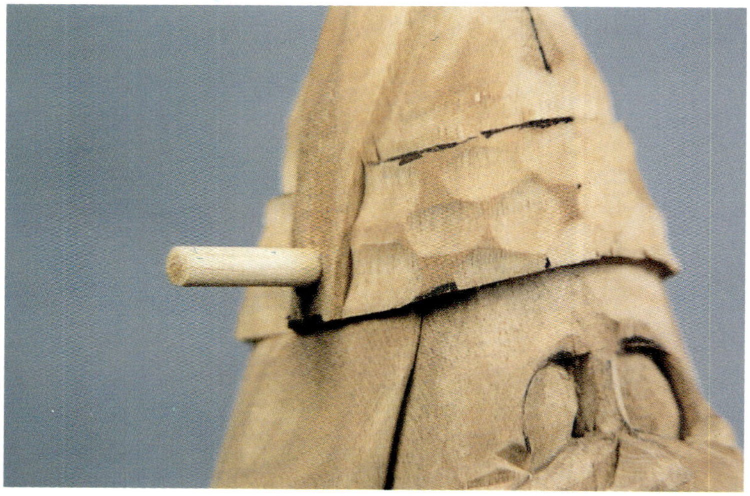

Now, insert (glue) a short section of 1/8" diameter wooden dowel into the hole in the hat, leaving about 1" protruding.

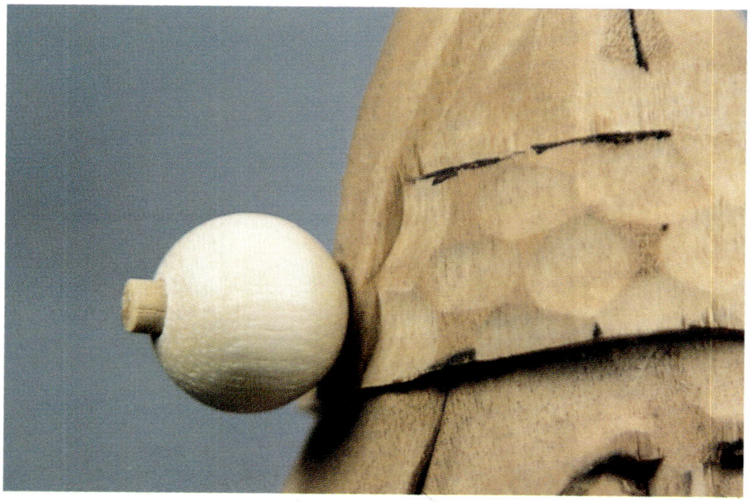

Select a wooden bead that looks like the right size to you. I normally keep bags of different size beads handy. Put a small dot of glue on the dowel, and slide the bead onto it until it sits flush against the hat.

Let the glue dry for about four hours, then use your knife to carefully cut away the excess dowel protruding from the outside of the bead. Trim as necessary so the outer edge of the bead will be smooth.

Painting the Project

The face and lip are FLESHTONE. While the paint is still damp, lightly blend in a small amount of BLUSH FLESH on the cheeks, nose and lip to give a slight "windburned" effect.

The eyes are TITANIUM WHITE. When the WHITE is dry, use a small, fine-tip brush and put a round dot of BABY BLUE in the upper right of the eyes. When this is dry, use your fine-tip brush to put a LAMP BLACK dot inside the BLUE dot. The placement of the BLUE and BLACK dots will have various effects on the facial expressions. Experiment on a piece of scrap wood to discover all the expressions you can create. I personally like to show the eyes rolled upward, looking toward one side or the other. You may experiment with different looks and find one that you prefer also.

Now, use a fine-tip brush or toothpick to place a TITANIUM WHITE highlight in the eyes.

Paint the eyebrows, hair, and beard using undiluted TITANIUM WHITE.

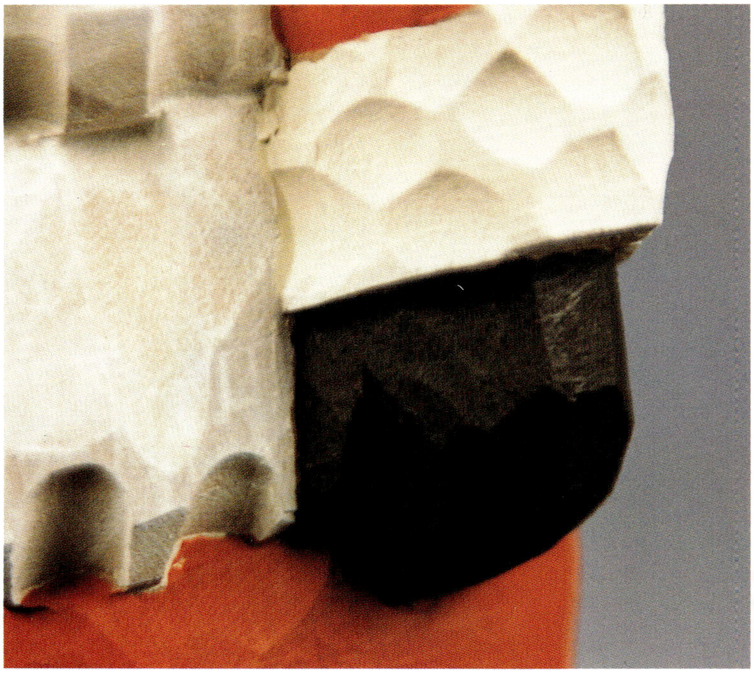

Paint the mittens LAMP BLACK, or a color of your choice.

Paint all the fur areas and pompom BUTTERMILK. Then, paint the hat and robe SANTA RED.

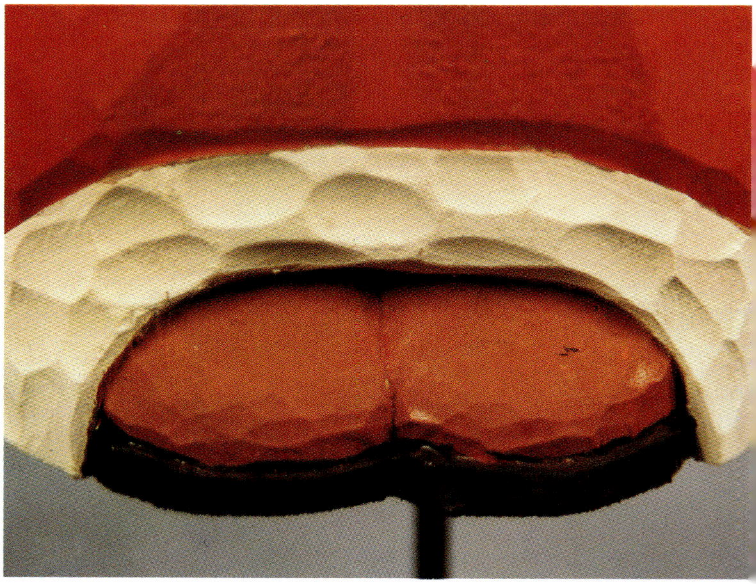

The soles of the shoes are BURNT UMBER, and the upper part of the shoes is RED IRON OXIDE.

Front view of completed project.

Left side view of completed project.

Rear view of completed project.

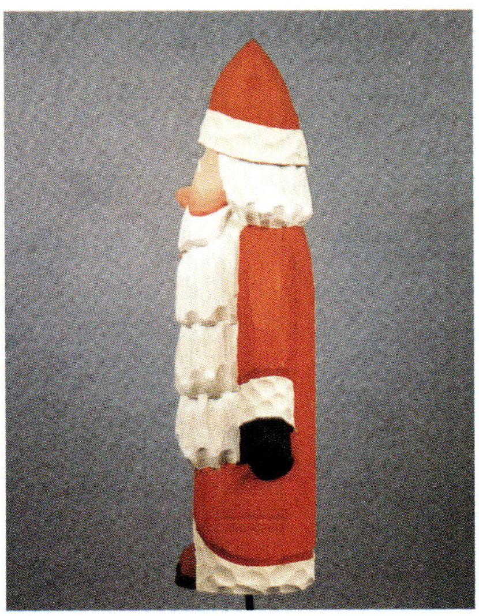

Right side view of completed project.

"Antiquing" the Project

Once the paint is dry, you may want to "age" your carving with an antiquing product in order to help tone down the colors a bit. I have had excellent results using antiquing gels made by DecoArt. These are available at hobby and craft stores. They come in various colors so you can create different effects.

Brush a coat of antiquing gel on the wood, then wipe it off using a damp rag or sponge. It is your option how much you wipe off. After the antiquing is dry, I like to finish my carvings with a coat of brush-on acrylic varnish. DecoArt also makes an excellent varnish. I prefer the one that leaves a satin finish. This particular finish is neither too flat nor too glossy, but leaves a "soft" look to the completed carving. (I usually put a coat of varnish on the face, hands, and other flesh areas before I antique the carving). This will prevent these areas from absorbing too much antiquing color.

Gallery and Study Models

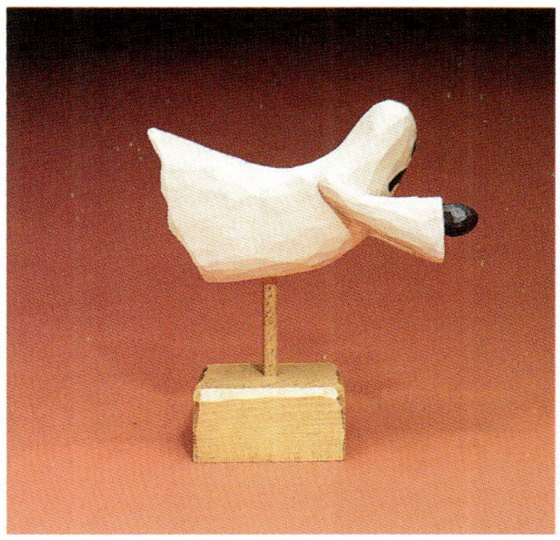

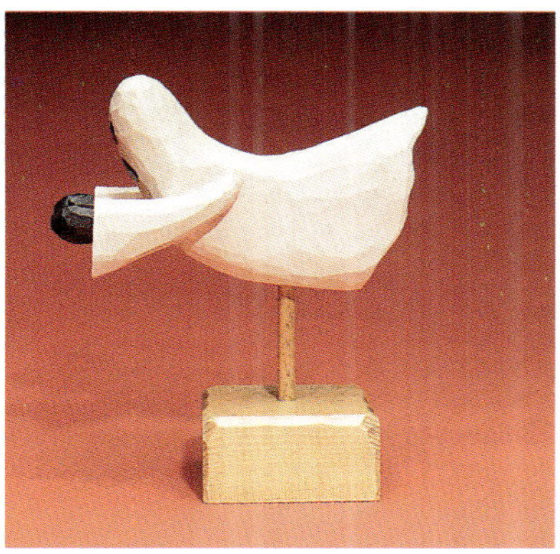

I hope that in some way I have been able to help each of you with some aspect of carving and painting. When we share tips and information, we all become better. If you have any comments or questions about something in this book, or if you have an idea you'd like to see me put in a future book, please feel free to write or call me at the following address and telephone number. I welcome any comments or suggestions you have.

Al Streetman
1609 N. Fordson Drive
Oklahoma City, Ok. 73127

Project Patterns

Christmas #1 (Carving Project Pattern)

2. St. Patrick's Day #1

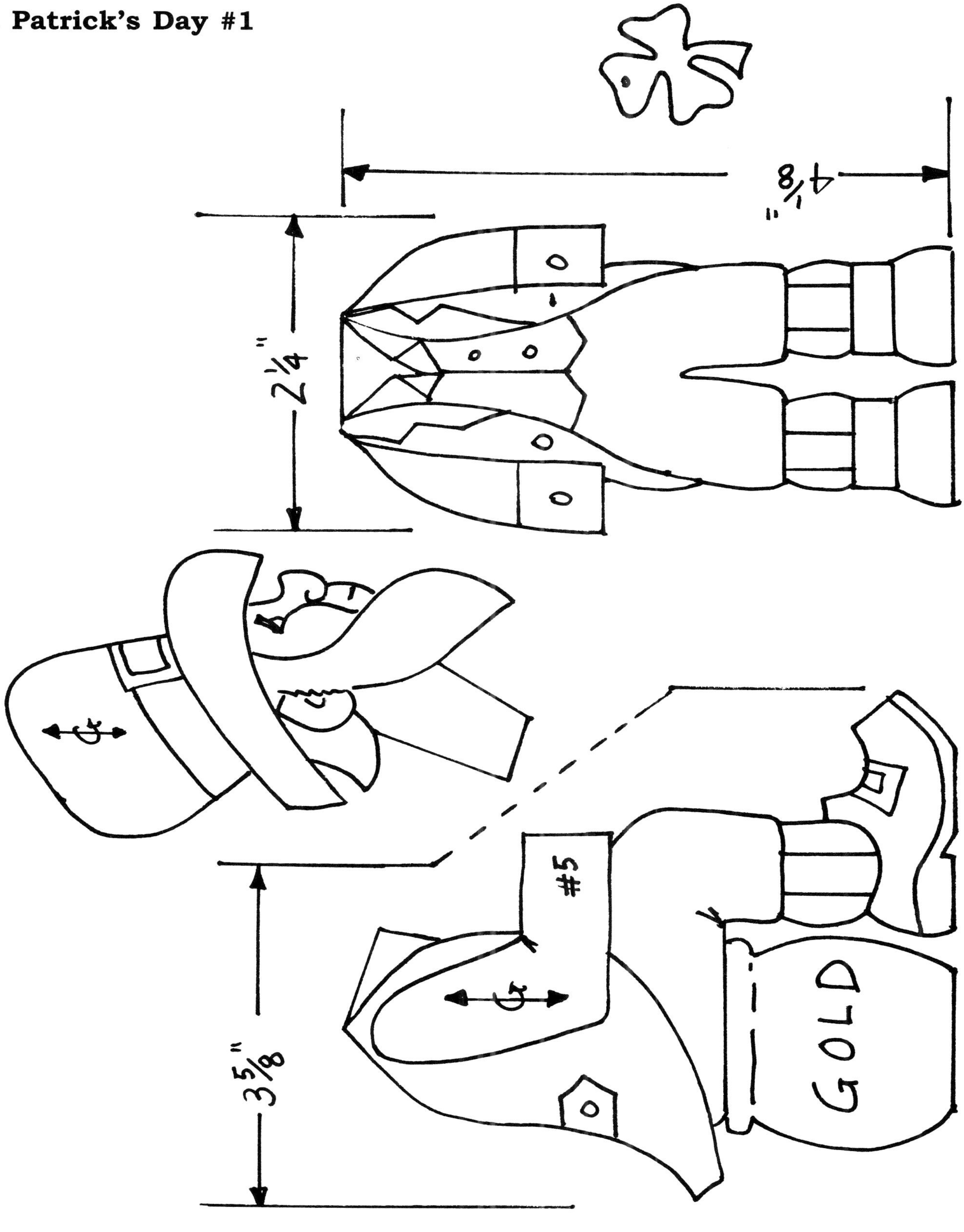

Refer to TIPS section for information about making fishing poles. Use a short piece of sewing thread for fish line.

St. Patrick's Day #2

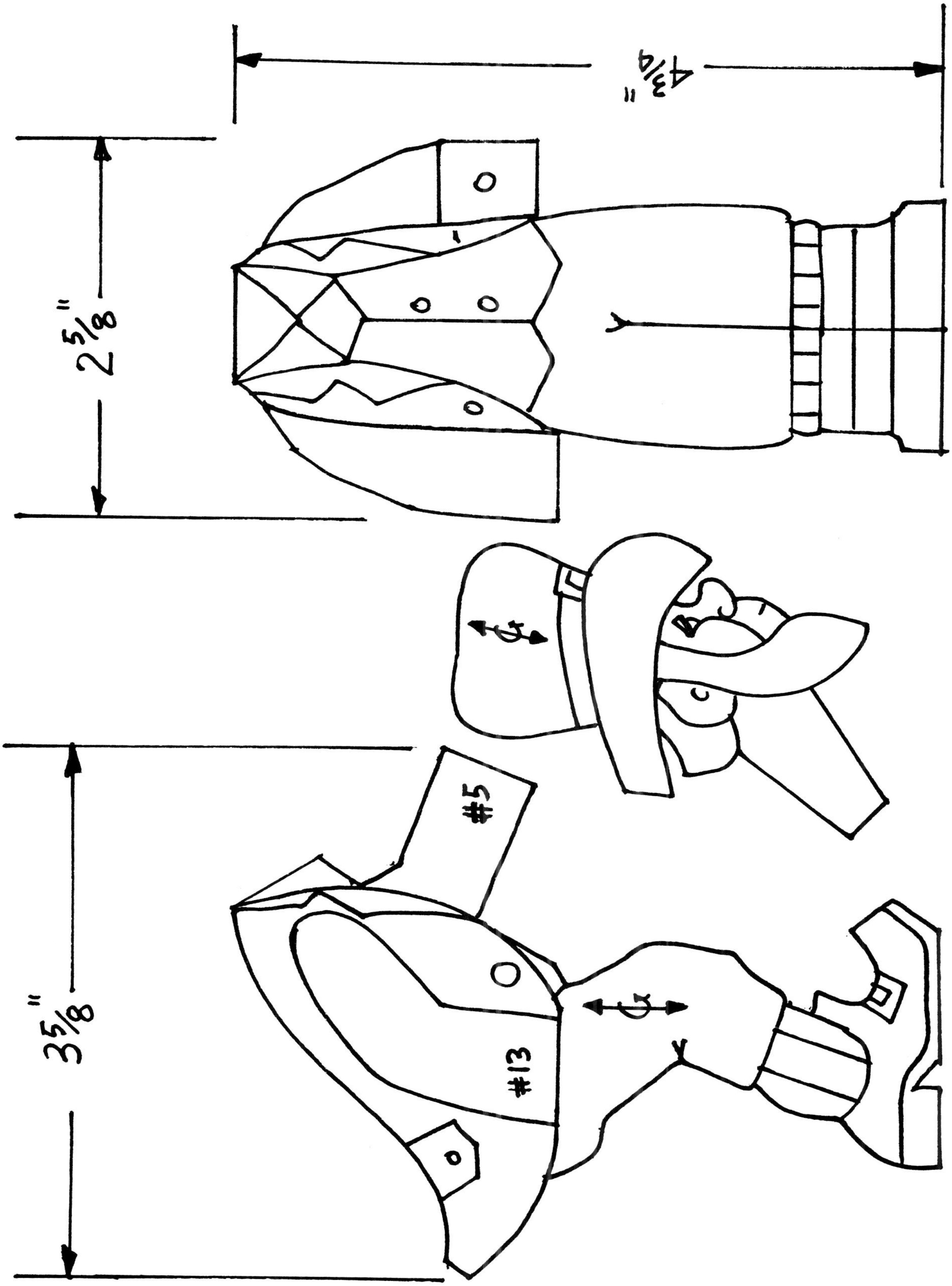

You may use this pattern for the walking stick, or use a twig.

St. Patrick's Day #3

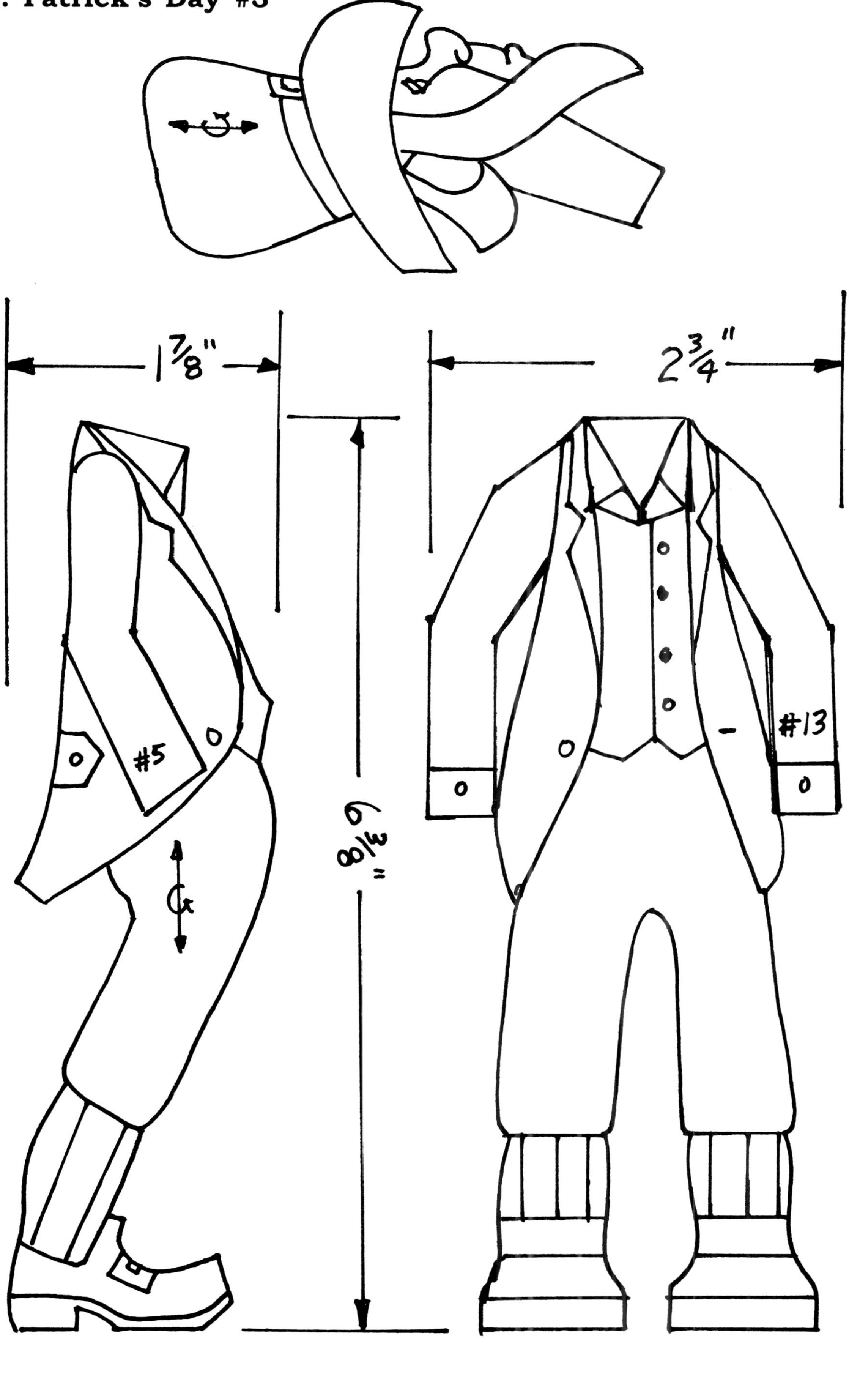

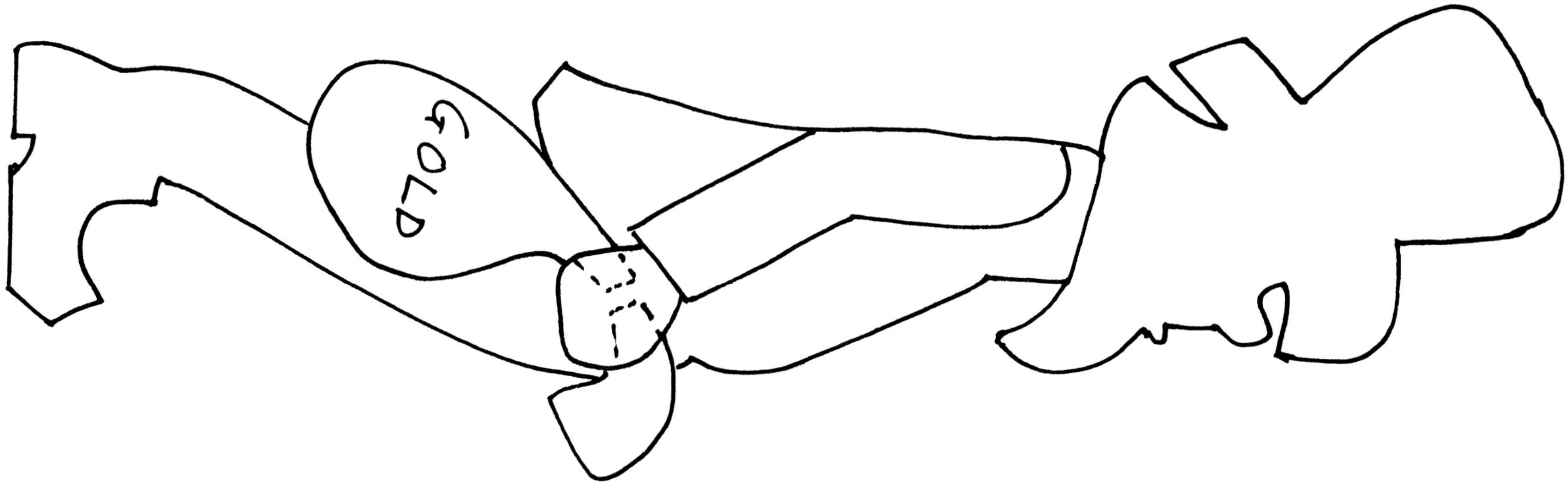

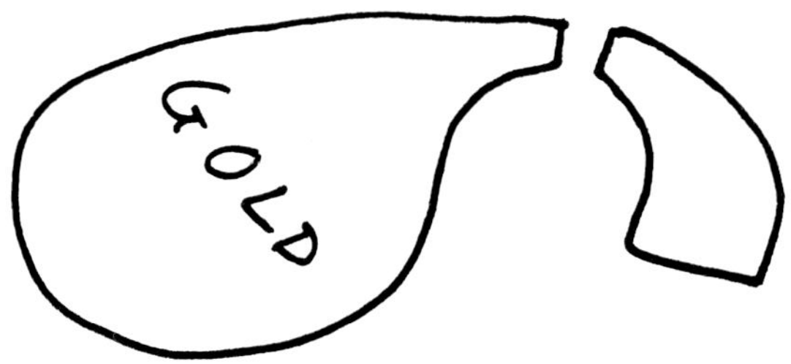

Saw out and carve gold bag as one piece. Then cut it apart as indicated, and glue the two sections into the hand.

Snowman #1

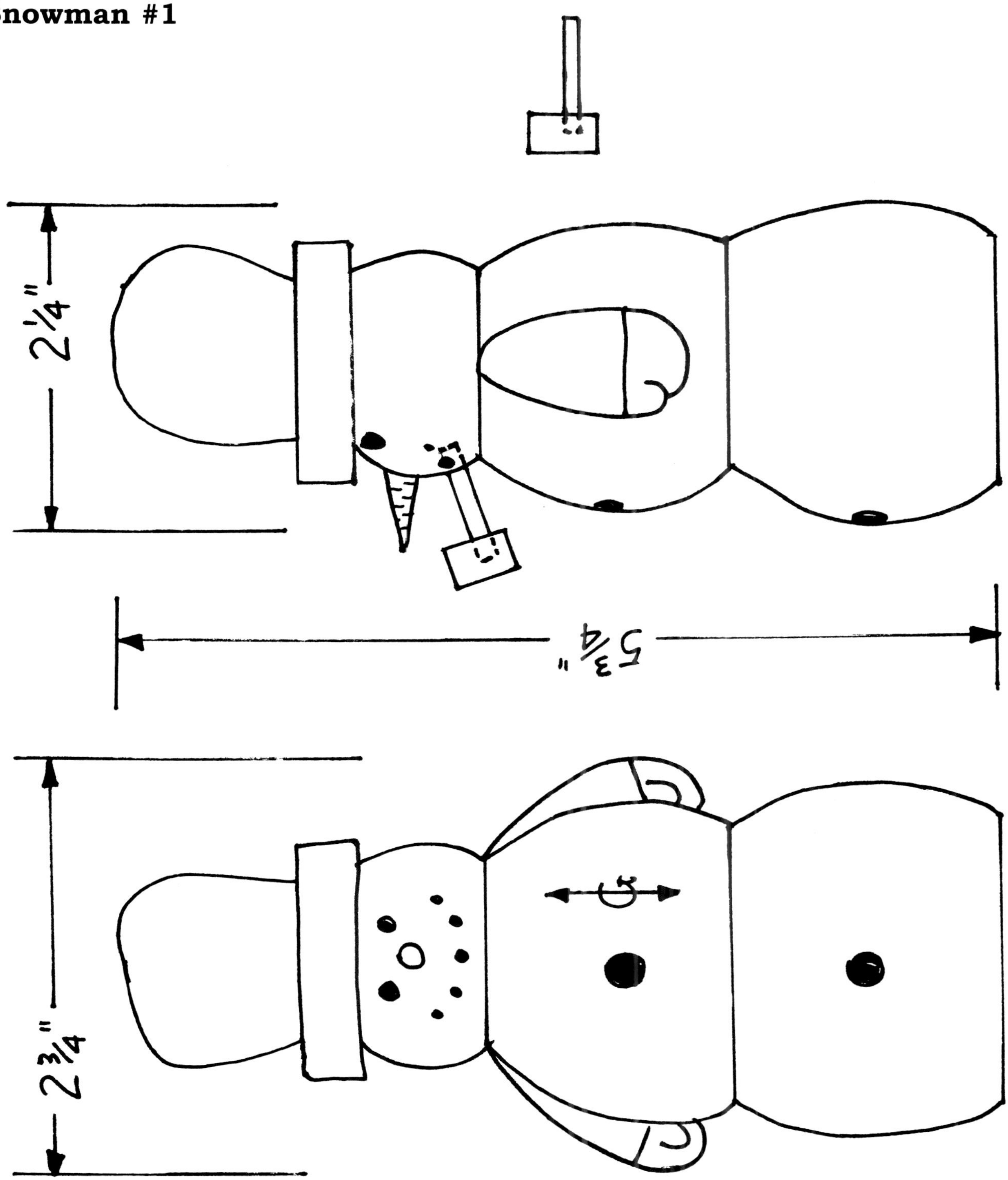

Snowman #2

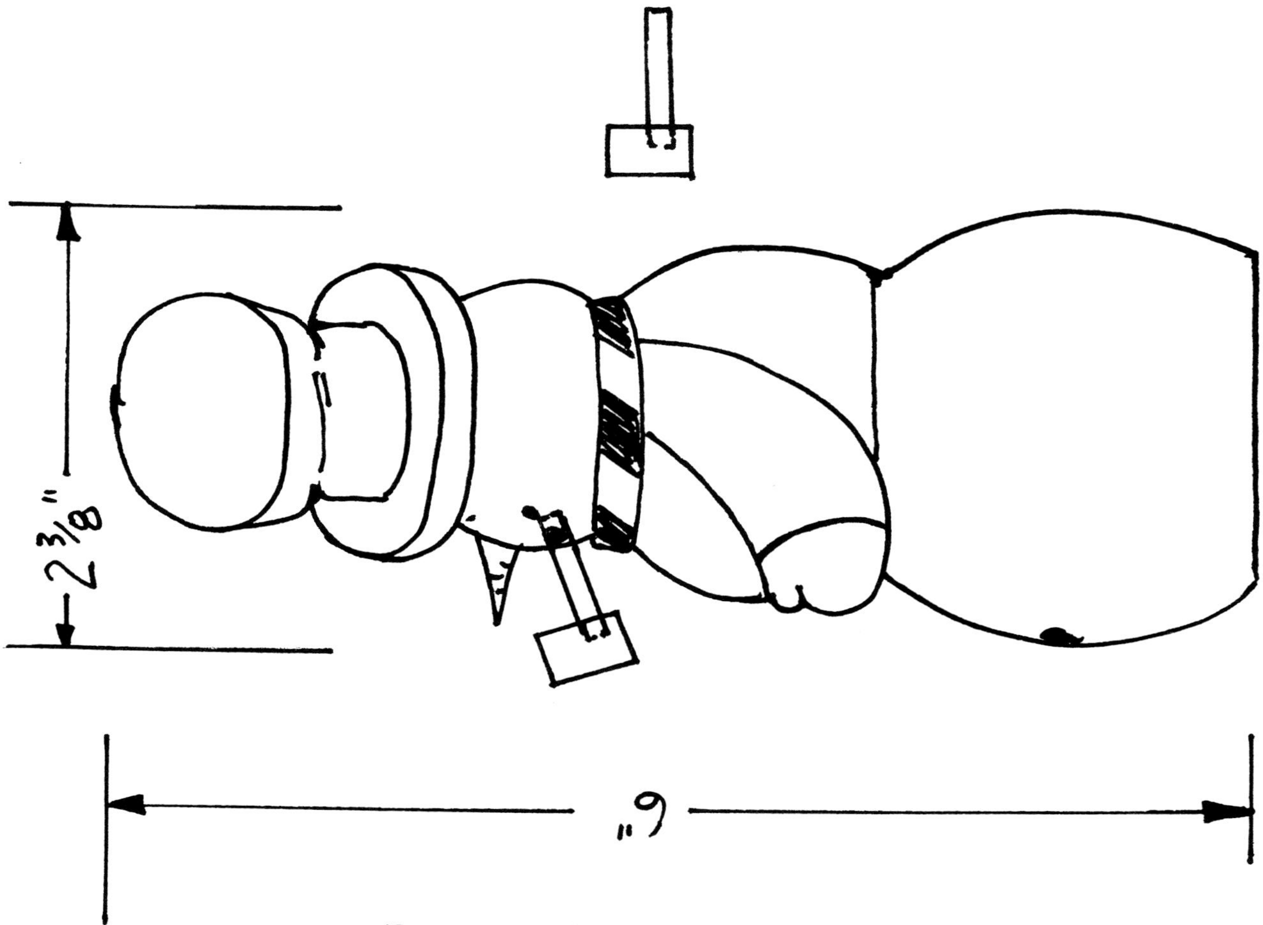

Paint scarf with colors
of your choice.

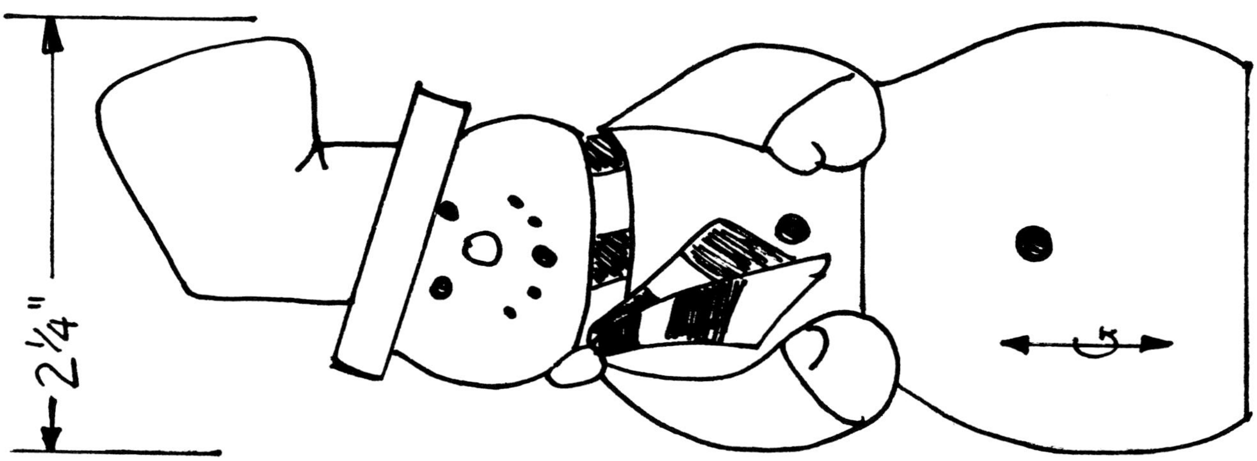

Snowman #3

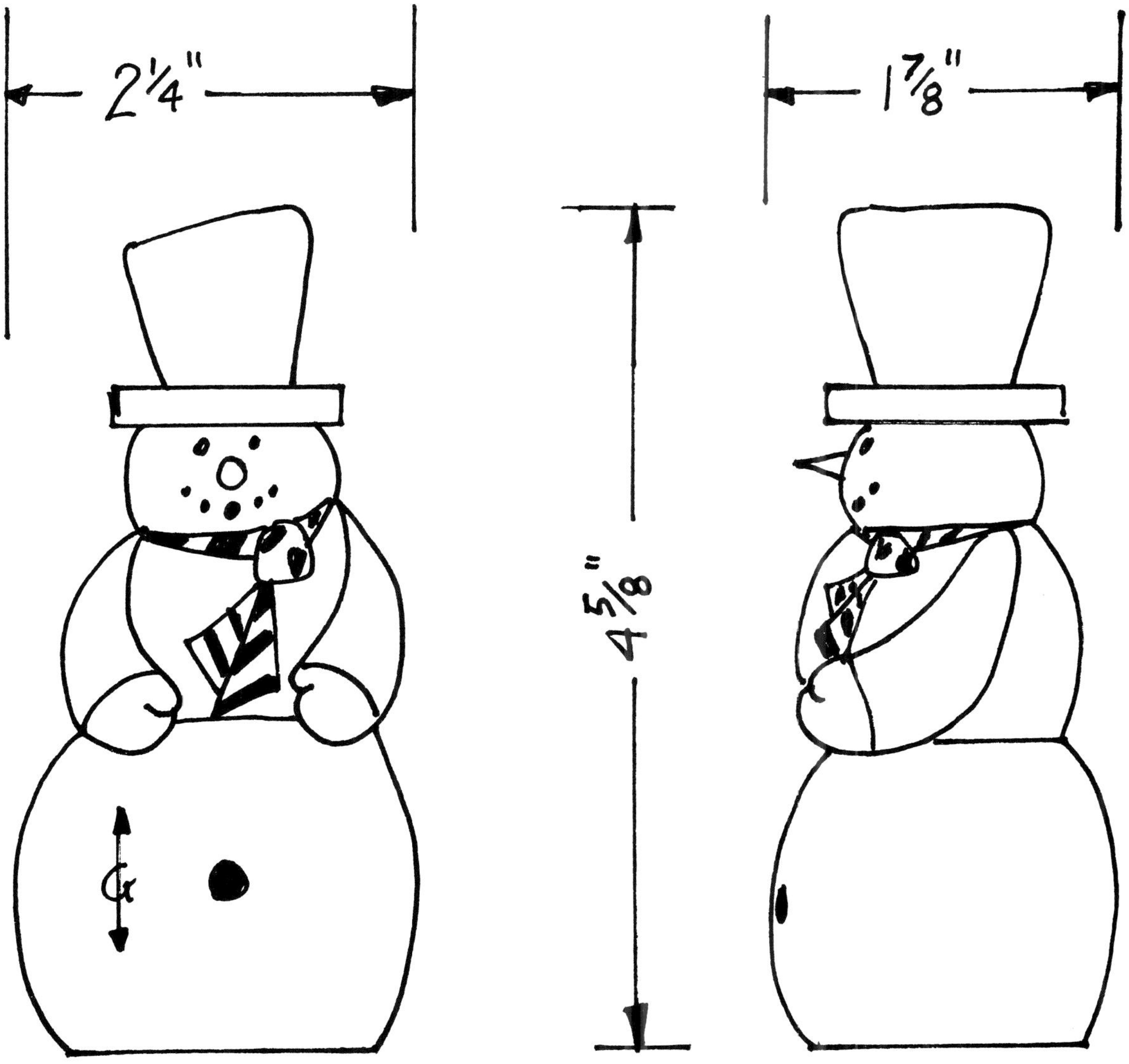

Snowman #4

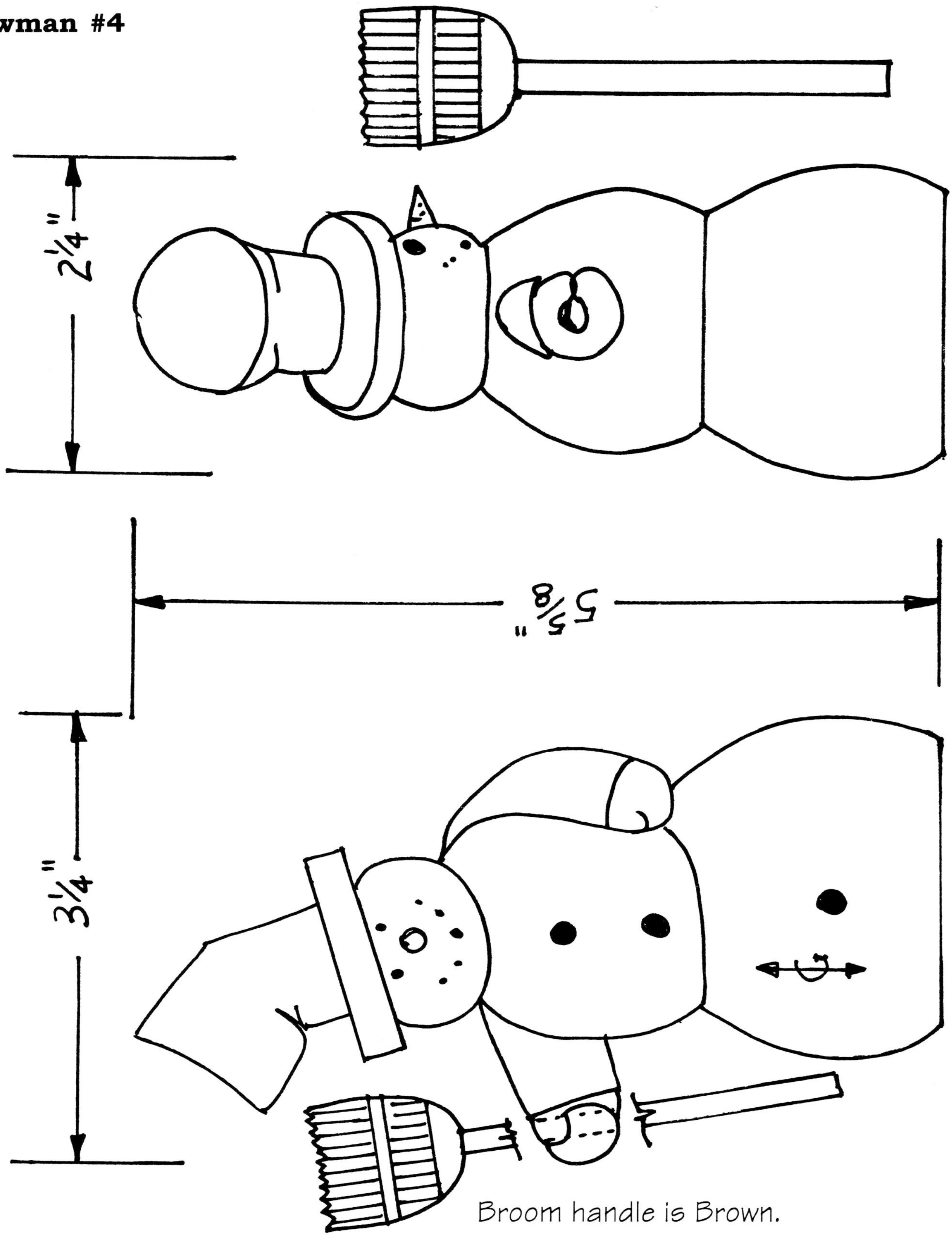

Broom handle is Brown.
Broom straws are Antique Gold.
Mittens are a color of your choice.

Snowman #5

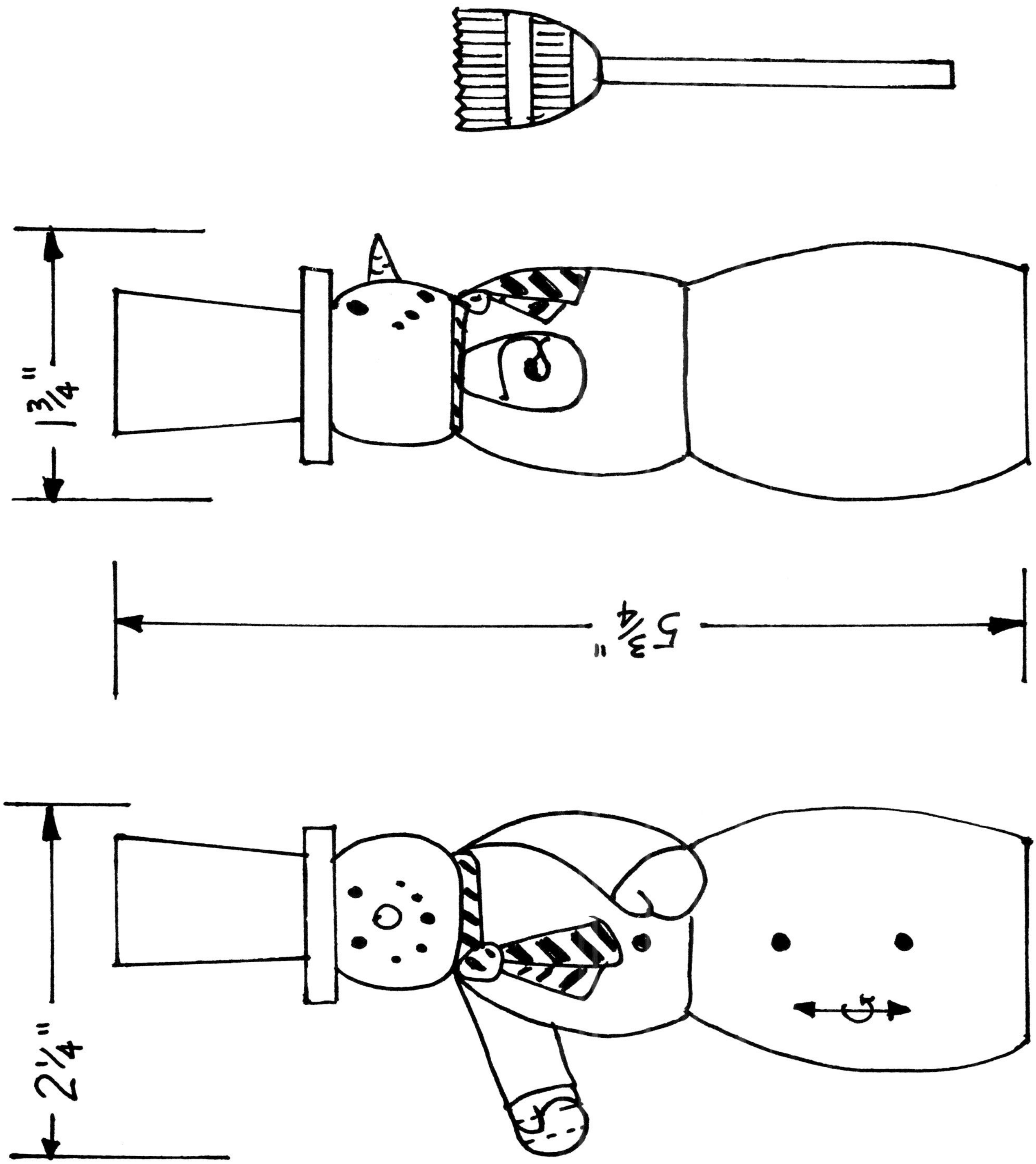

Halloween #1

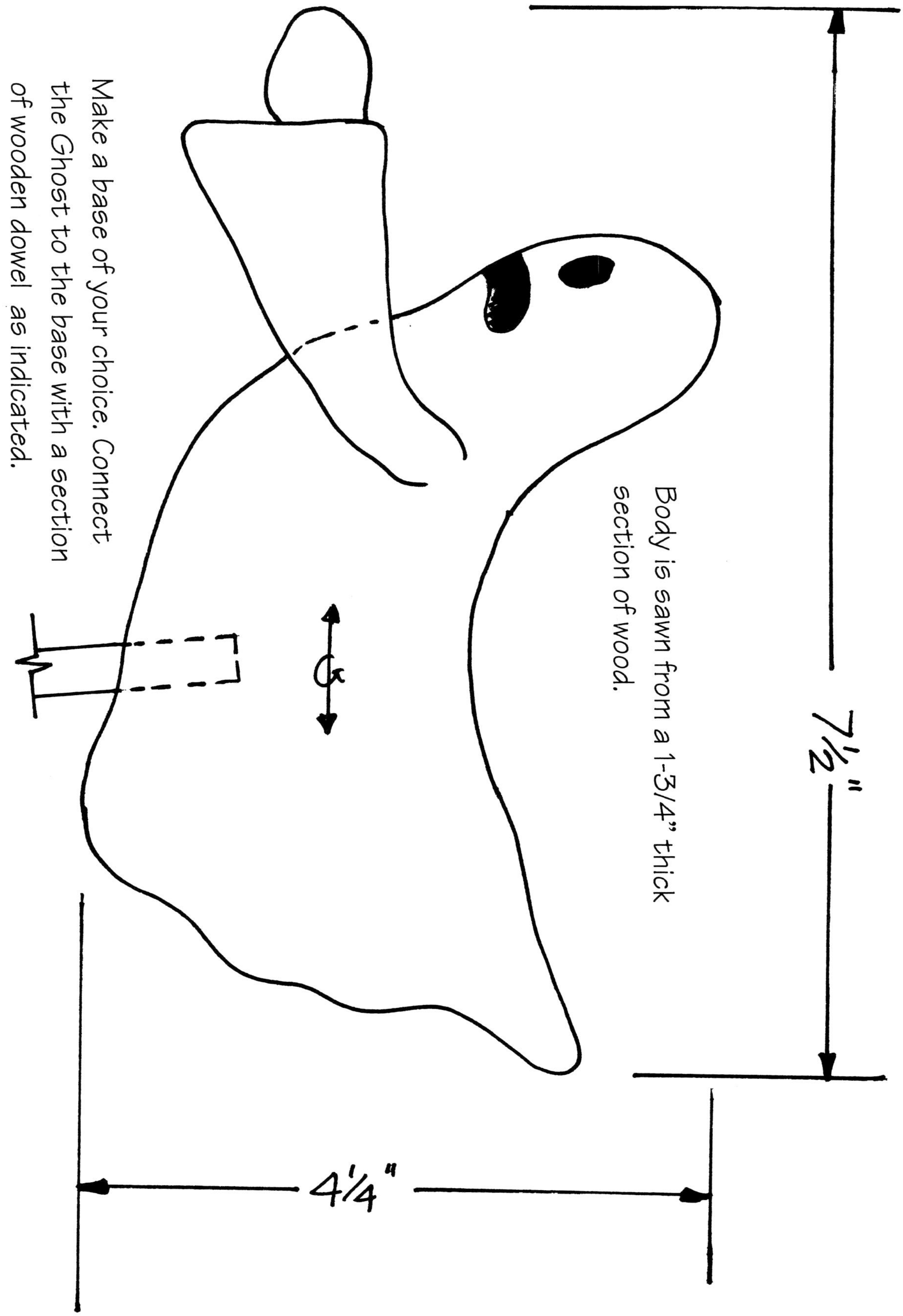
Make a base of your choice. Connect the Ghost to the base with a section of wooden dowel as indicated.
Body is sawn from a 1-3/4" thick section of wood.
7½"
4¼"

Halloween #2

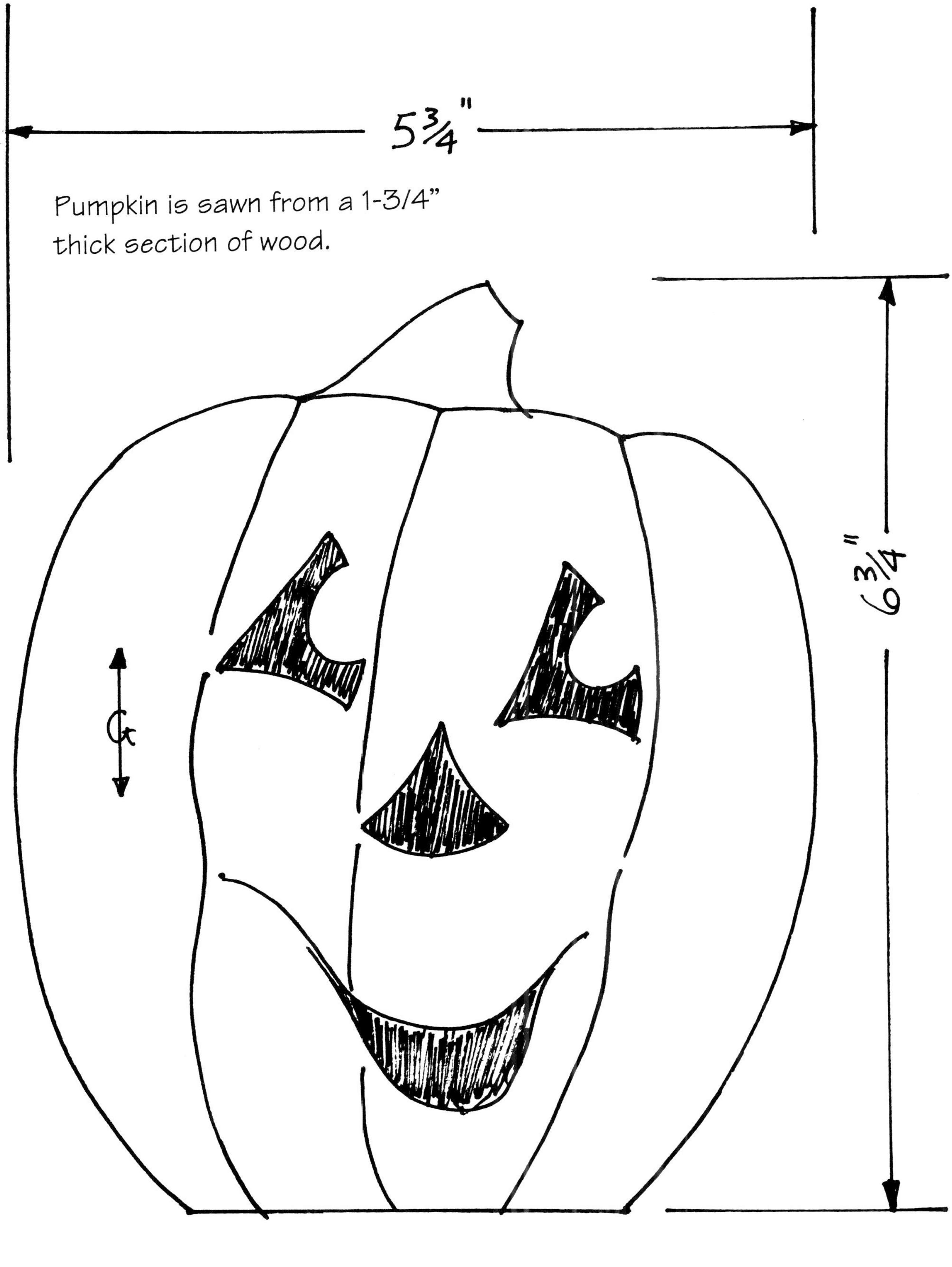

Halloween #3

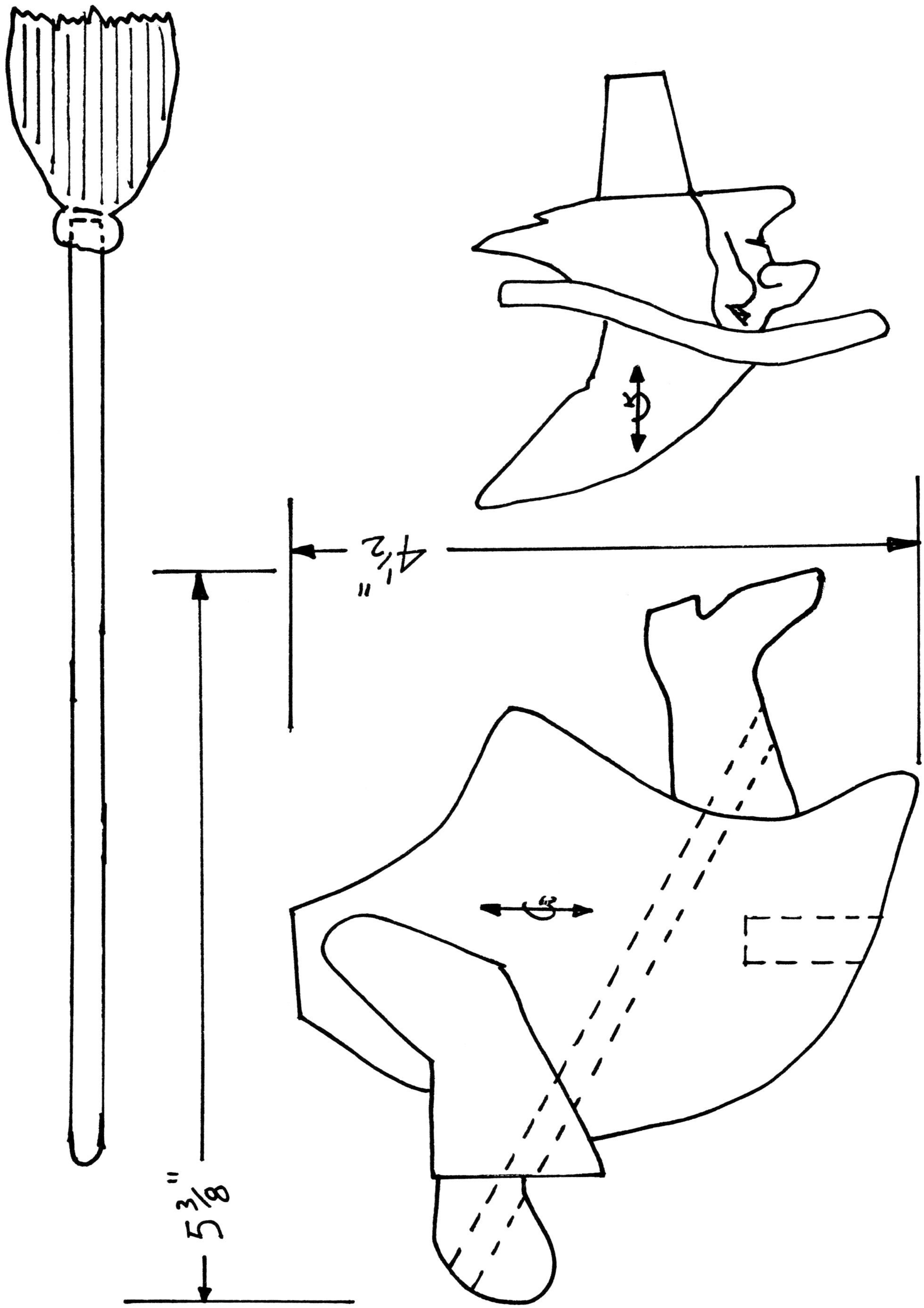

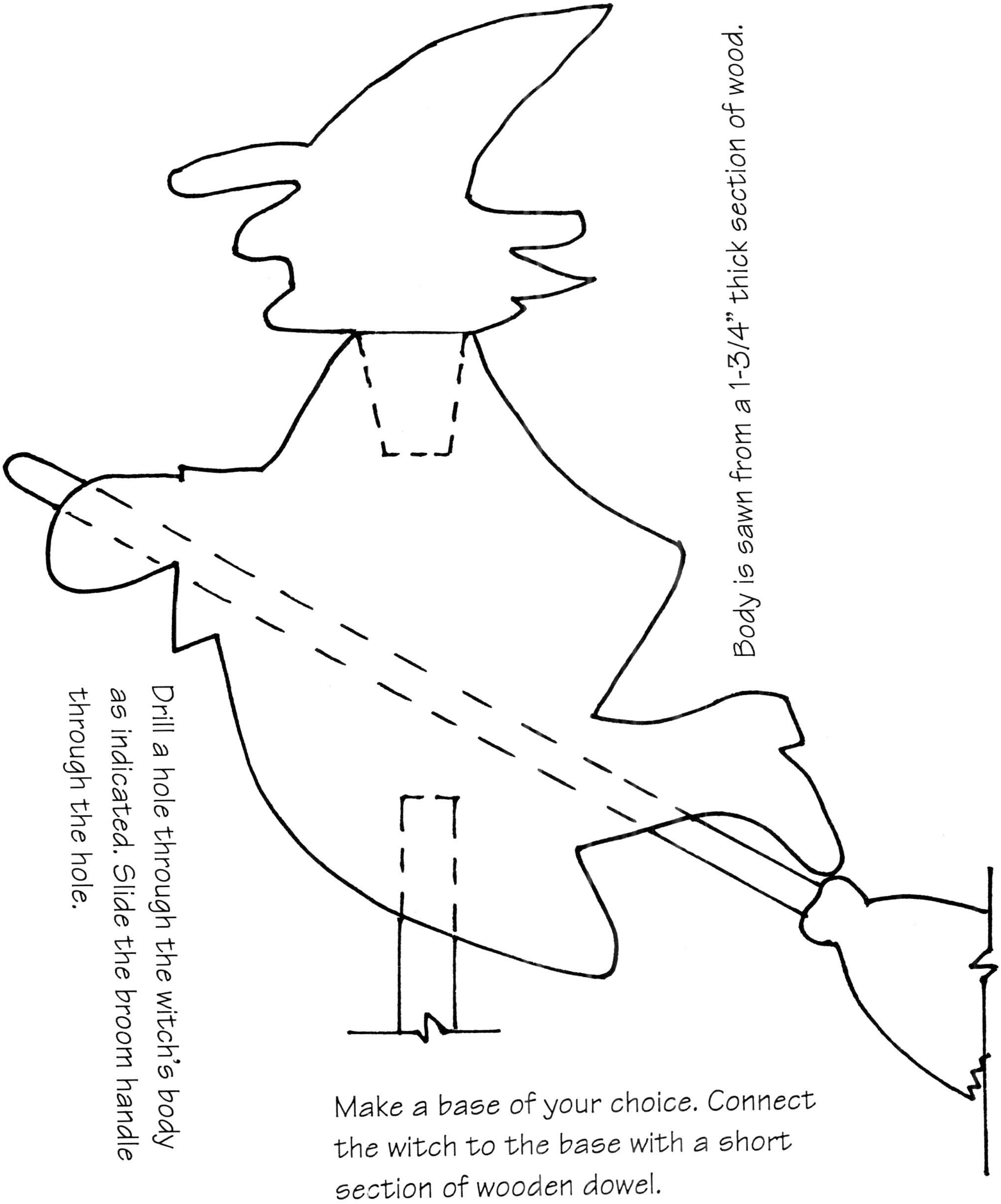

Body is sawn from a 1-3/4" thick section of wood.

Drill a hole through the witch's body as indicated. Slide the broom handle through the hole.

Make a base of your choice. Connect the witch to the base with a short section of wooden dowel.

Thanksgiving #1

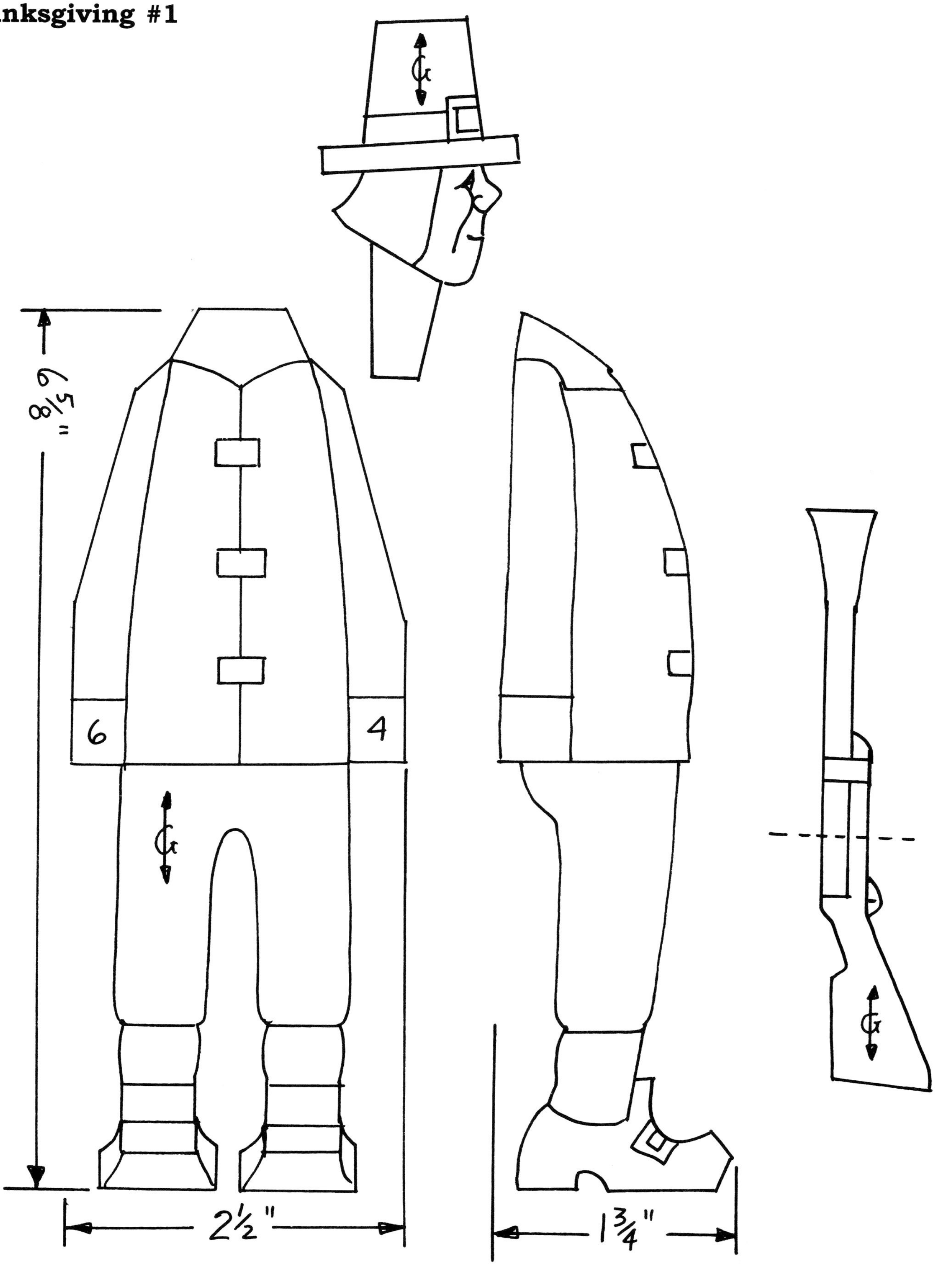

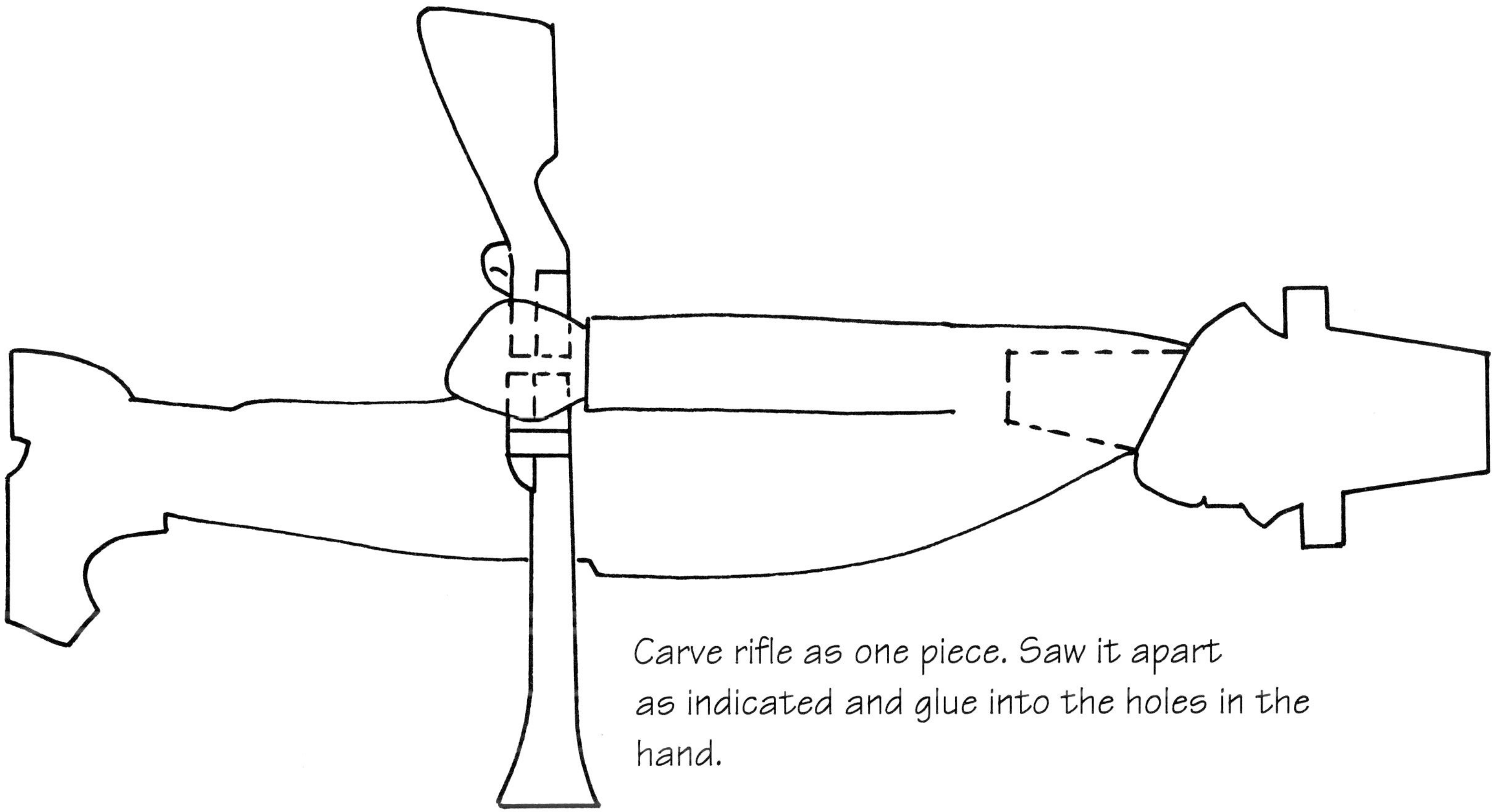

Carve rifle as one piece. Saw it apart as indicated and glue into the holes in the hand.

Thanksgiving #2

Thanksgiving #3

Fourth of July #1

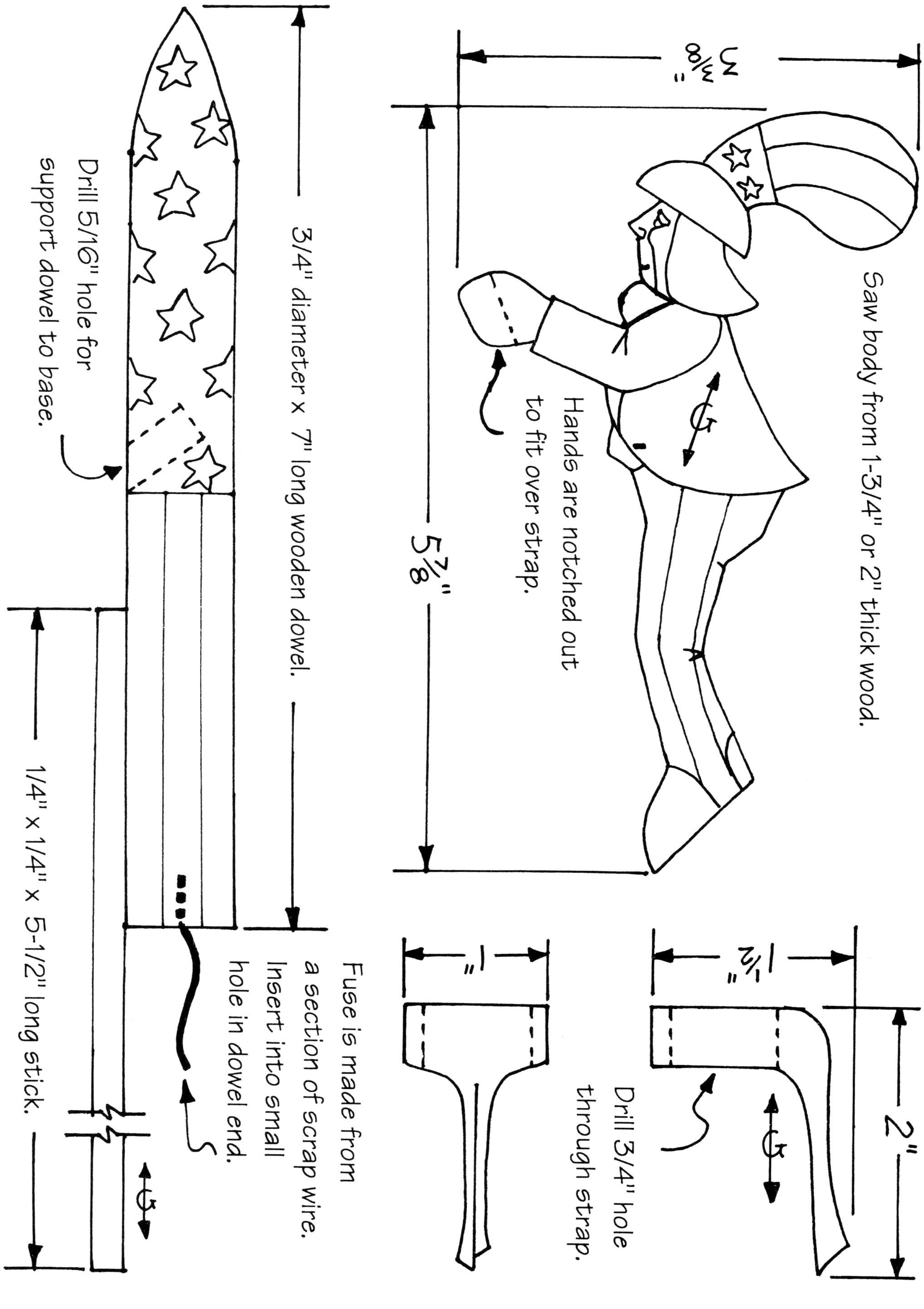

Make a base of your choice.

Drill a 5/16" hole in the base, and cut a short section of 5/16" wooden dowel.

Stain or paint the base and dowel a color of your choice, then glue the dowel into the base.

Attach the completed rocket to the base with the 5/16" dowel.

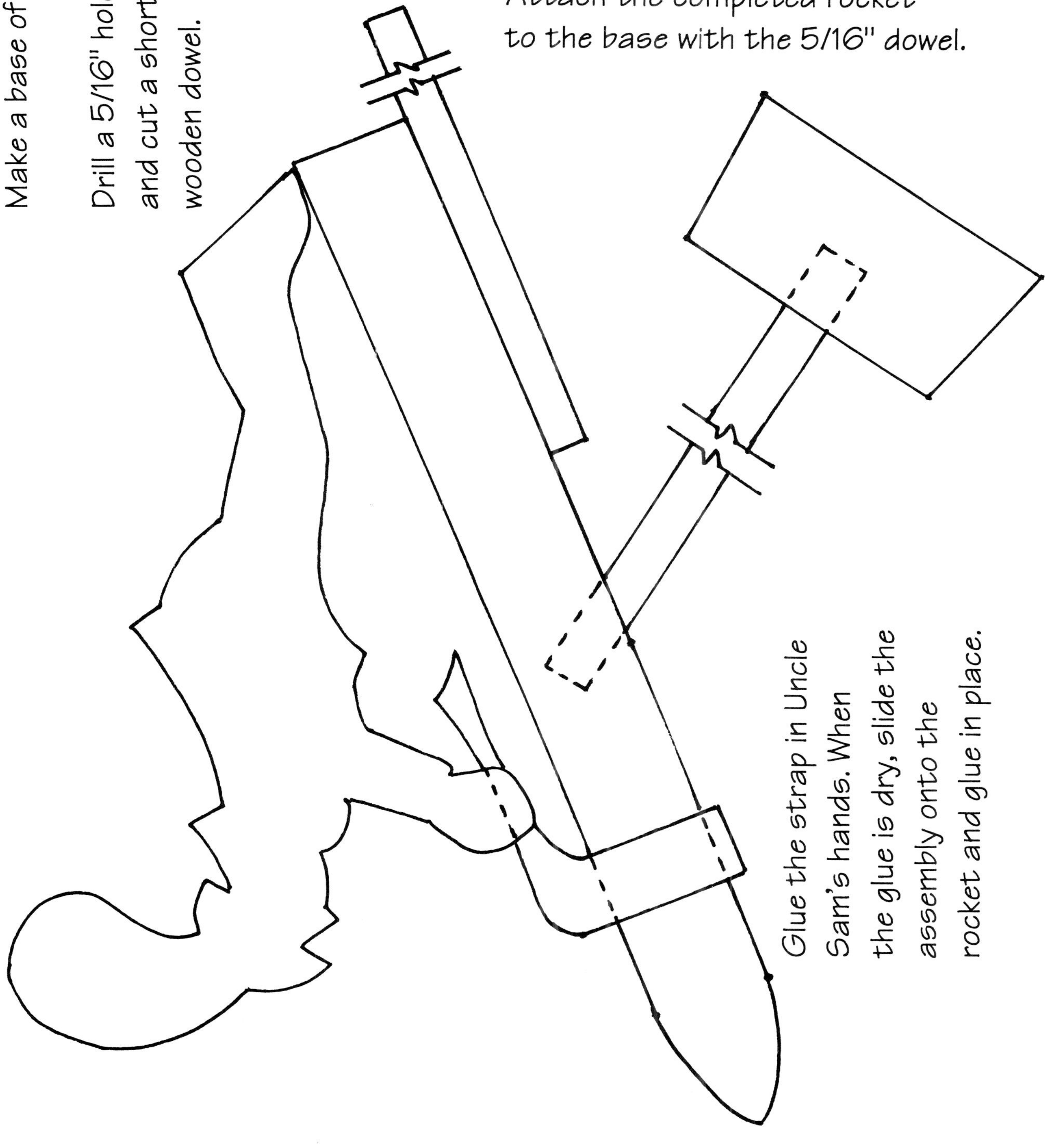

Glue the strap in Uncle Sam's hands. When the glue is dry, slide the assembly onto the rocket and glue in place.

Fourth of July #2

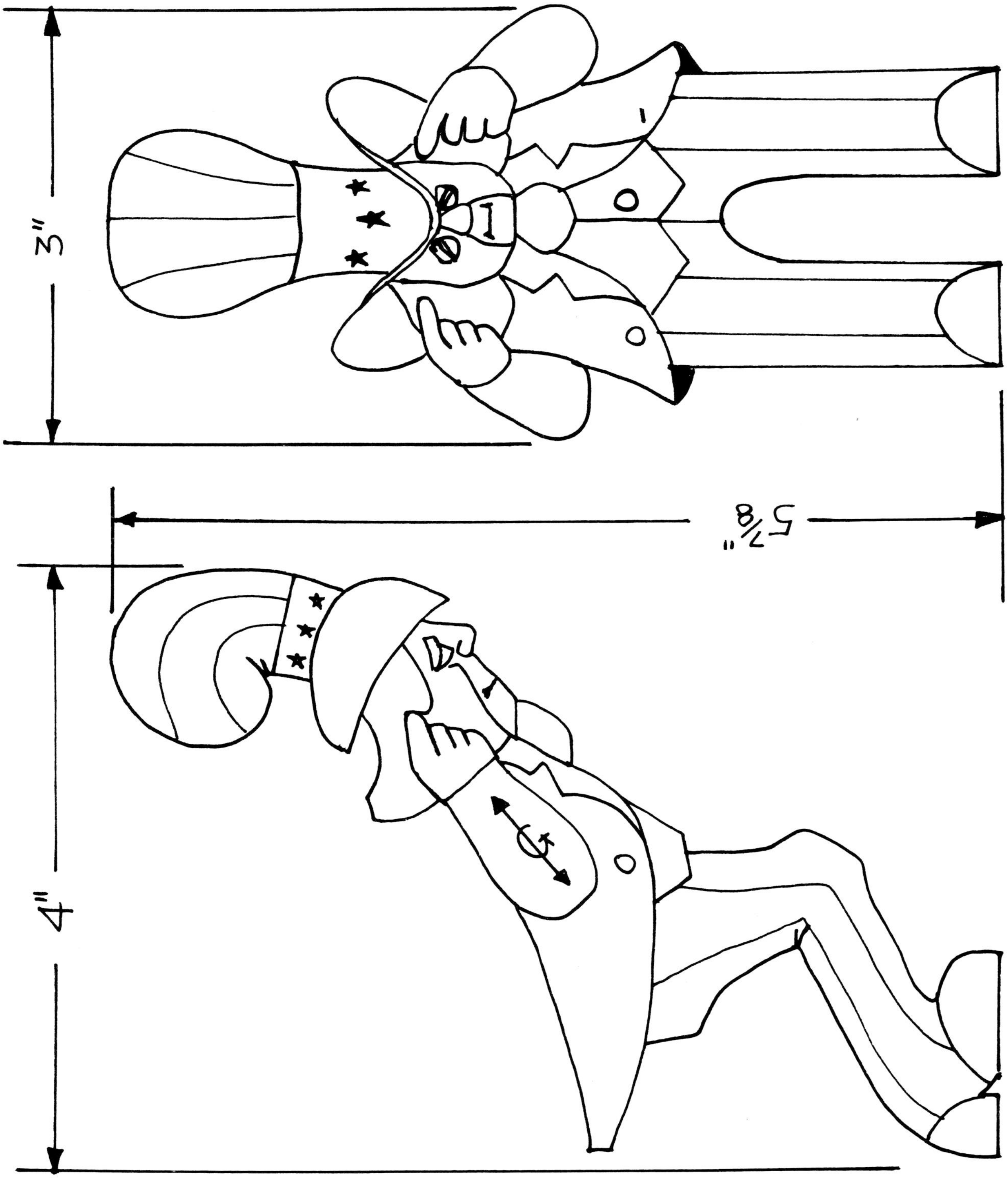

Firecracker is made from 3/4" diameter wooden dowel.

Base of firecracker is made from 1/4" thick scrap wood,
1-1/4" square.

Mount completed project on a base for
stability.

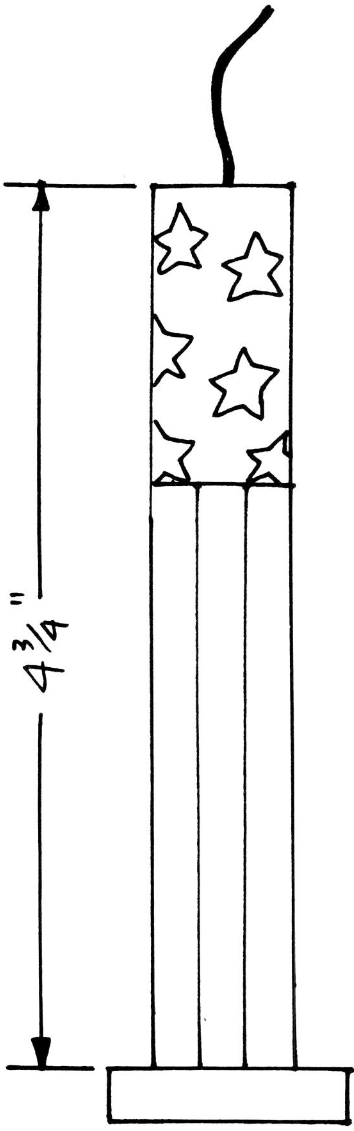

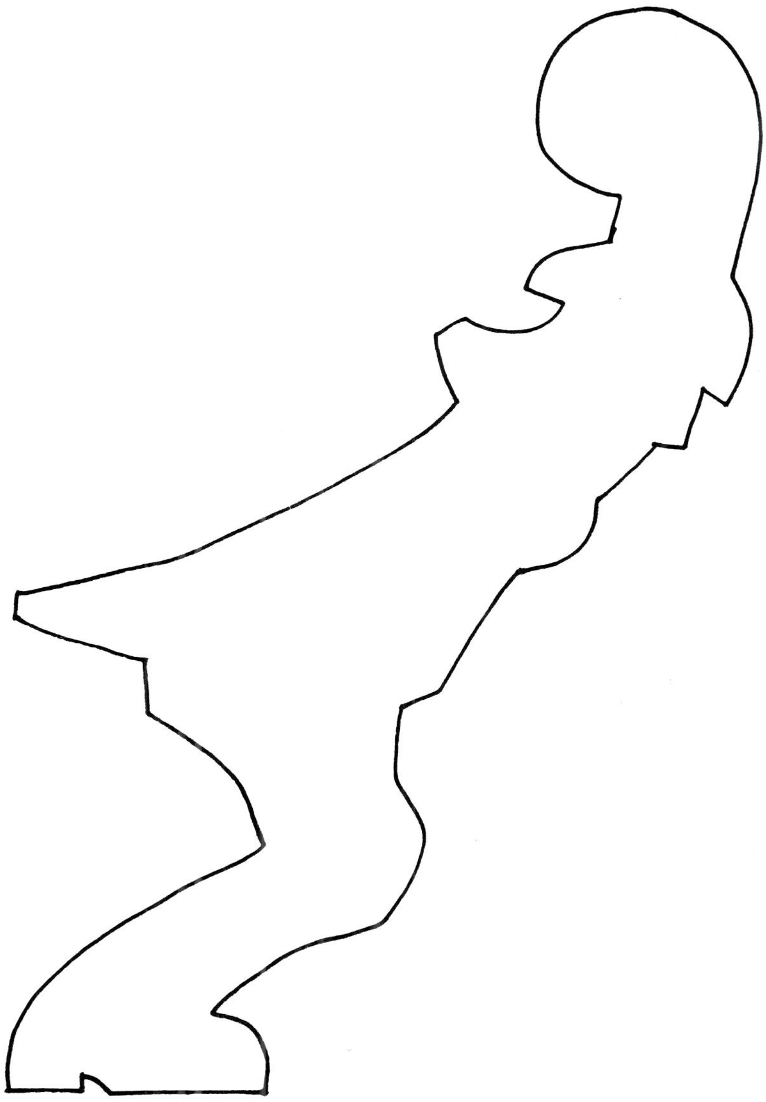

Fourth of July #3

Rocket is made from 3/16" diameter wooden dowel. Tail stick is made from a toothpick.

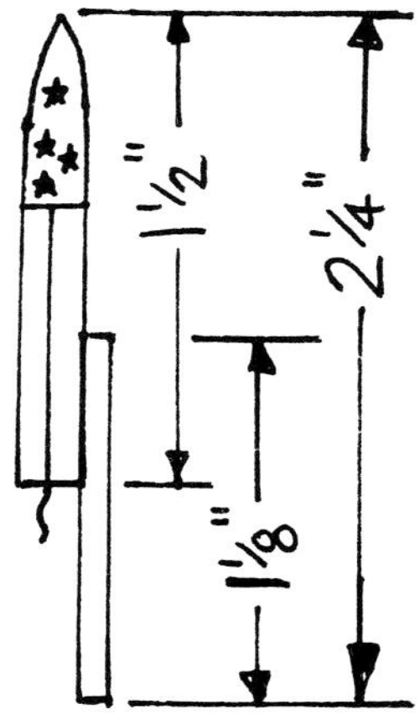

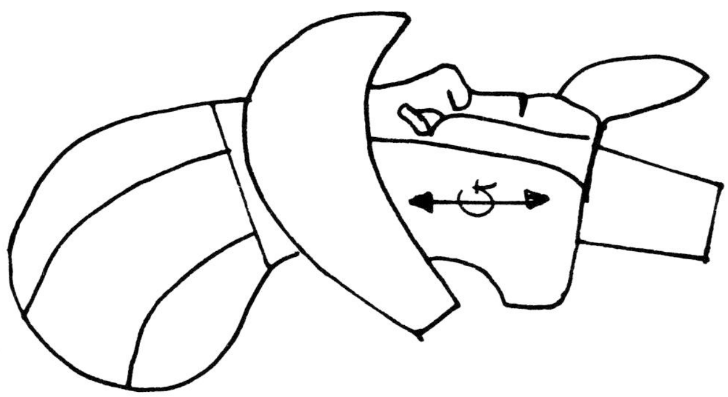

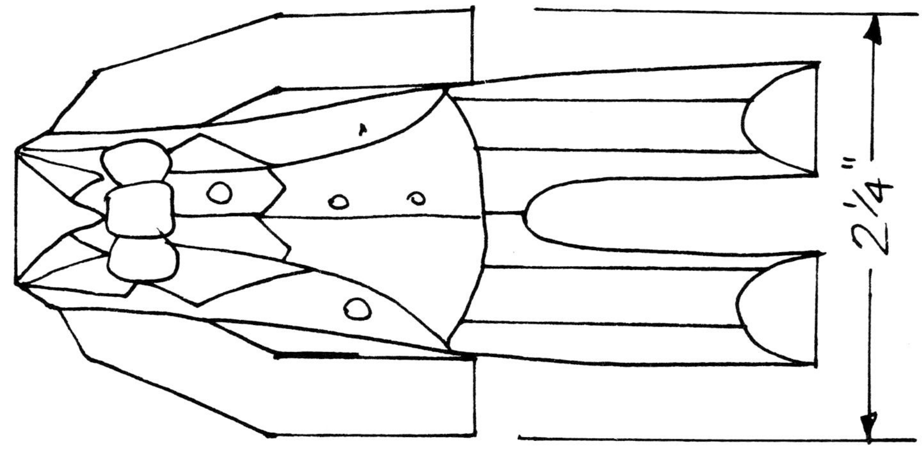

Use Hand # 6 for both hands. Drill 3/16" holes through the hands for the rocket and flag pole.

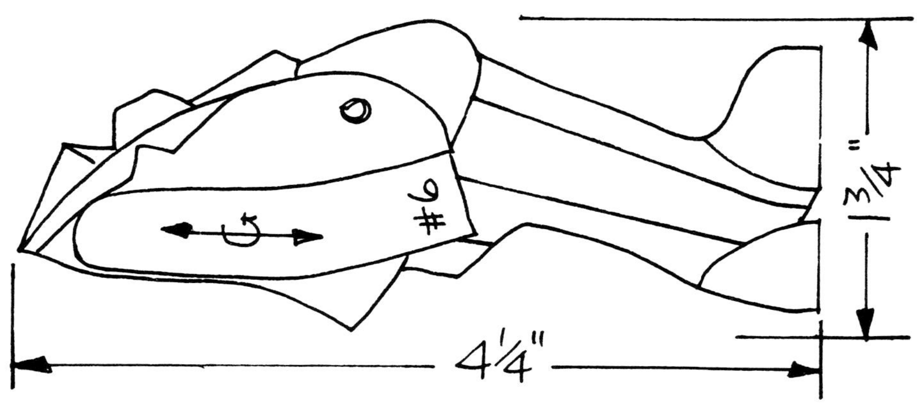

Flag pole is made from 3/16" diameter wooden dowel, 4-1/2" in length.
Drill hole in left hand at the approximate angle shown, so the flag will point up when inserted in the hand.

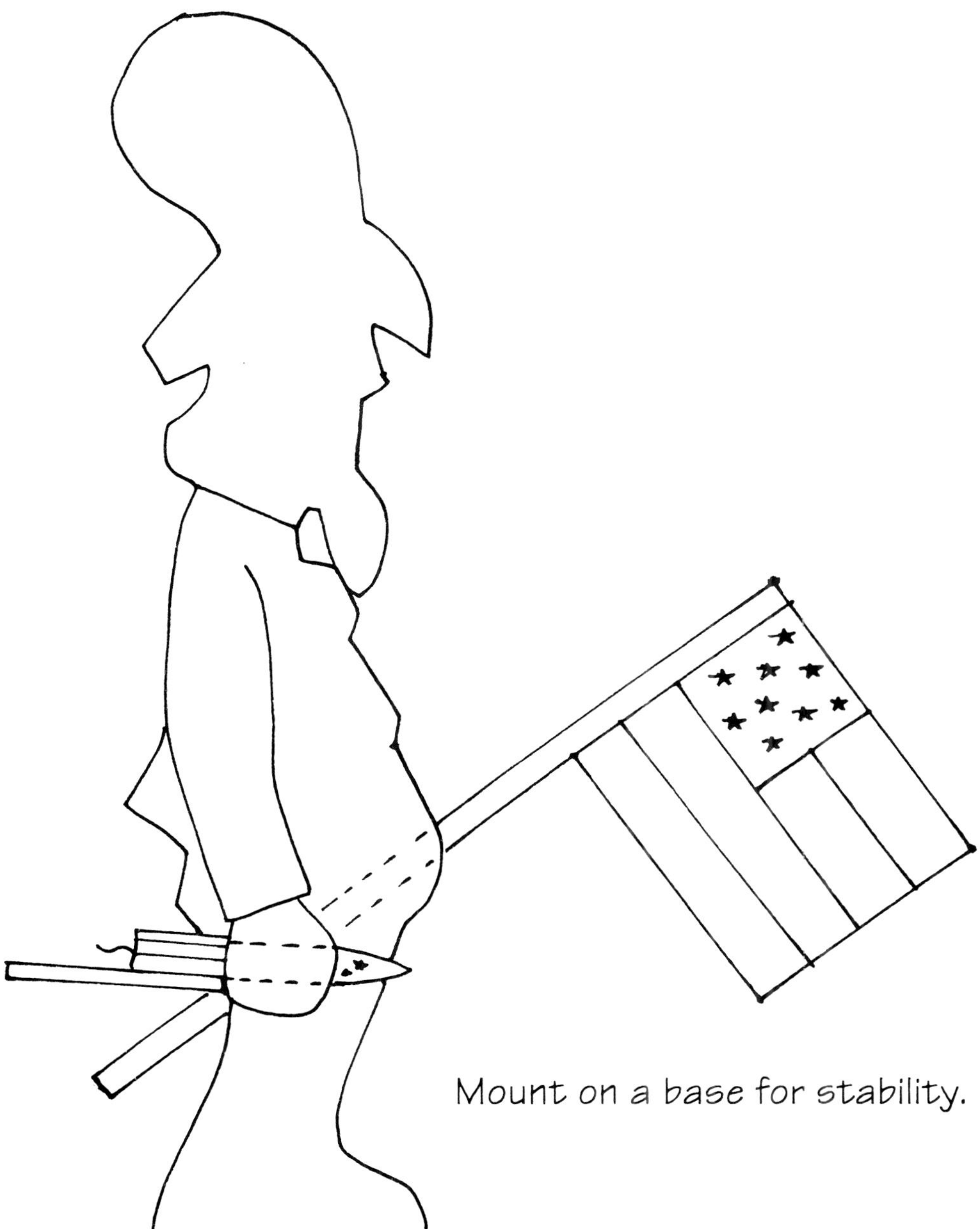

Mount on a base for stability.

Fourth of July #4

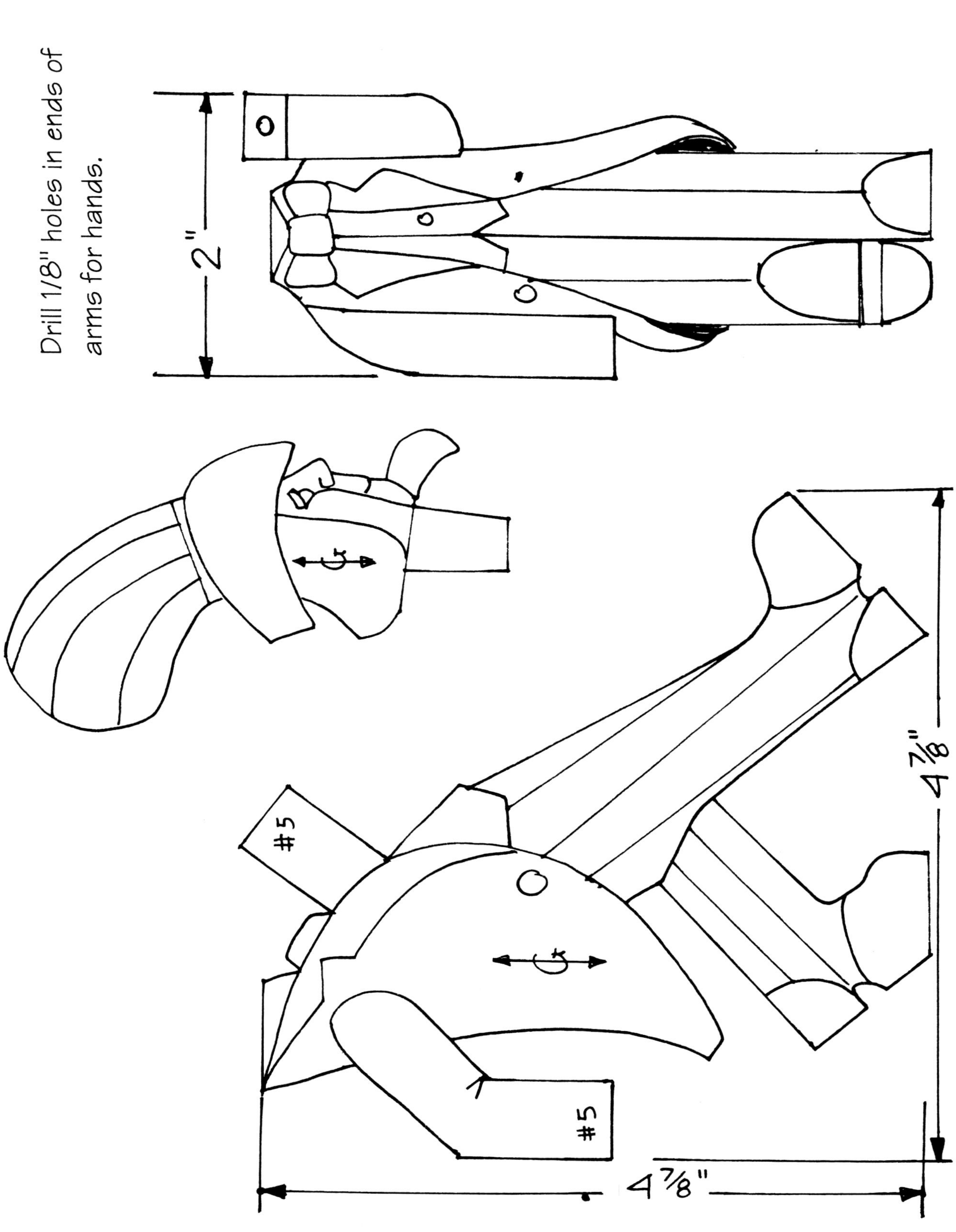

Construct firecrackers from 3/16" diameter wooden dowel, 1-1/2" in length.
Drill 3/16" holes through hands for firecrackers.

Mount on a base for stability.

Fourth of July #5

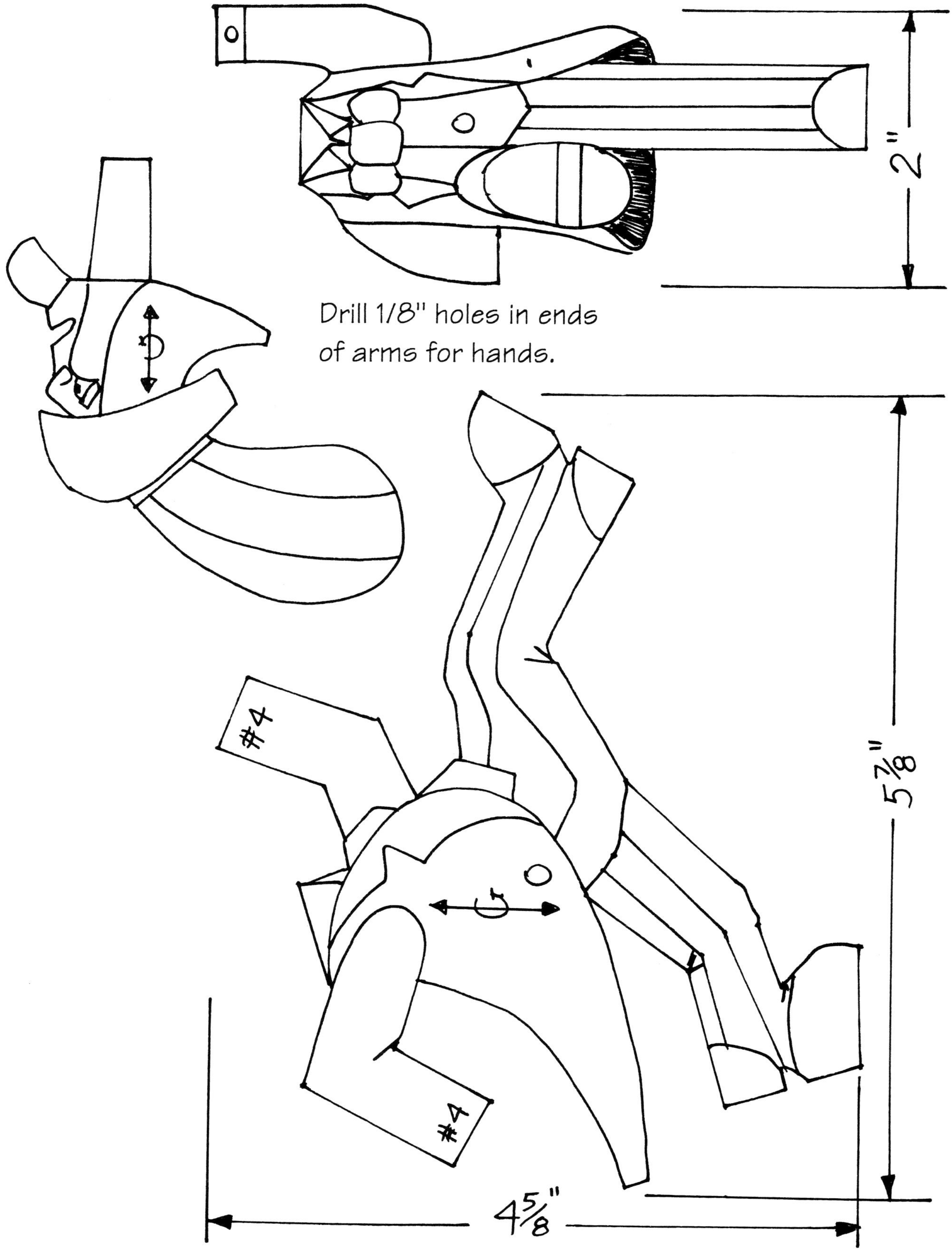

Firecracker is made from 1" diameter wooden dowel, 2-1/2" in length.
Base is made from 1-1/2" square scrap wood, 1/4" thick.

Mount finished carving on a base for stability.

Easter #1

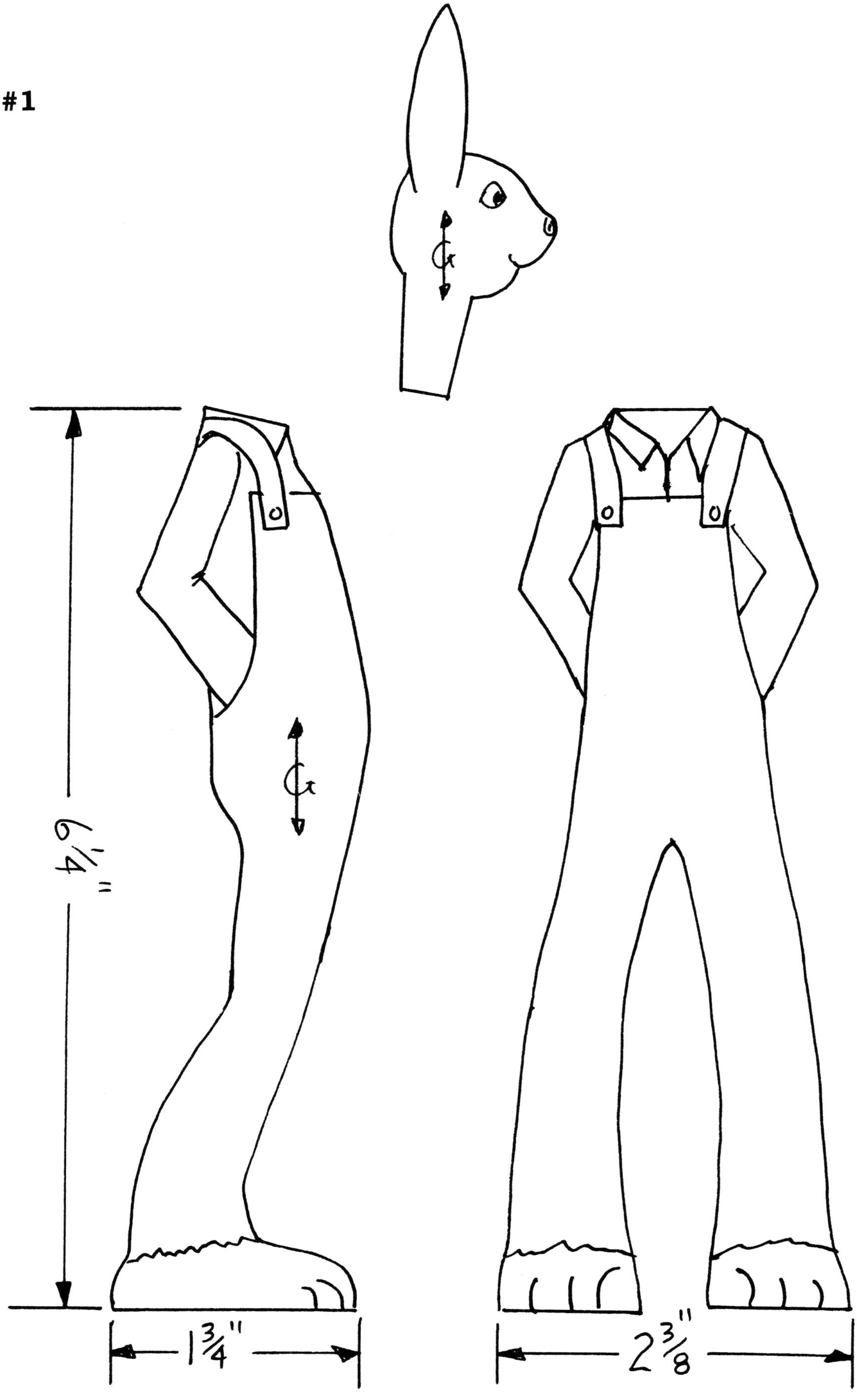

Easter #2

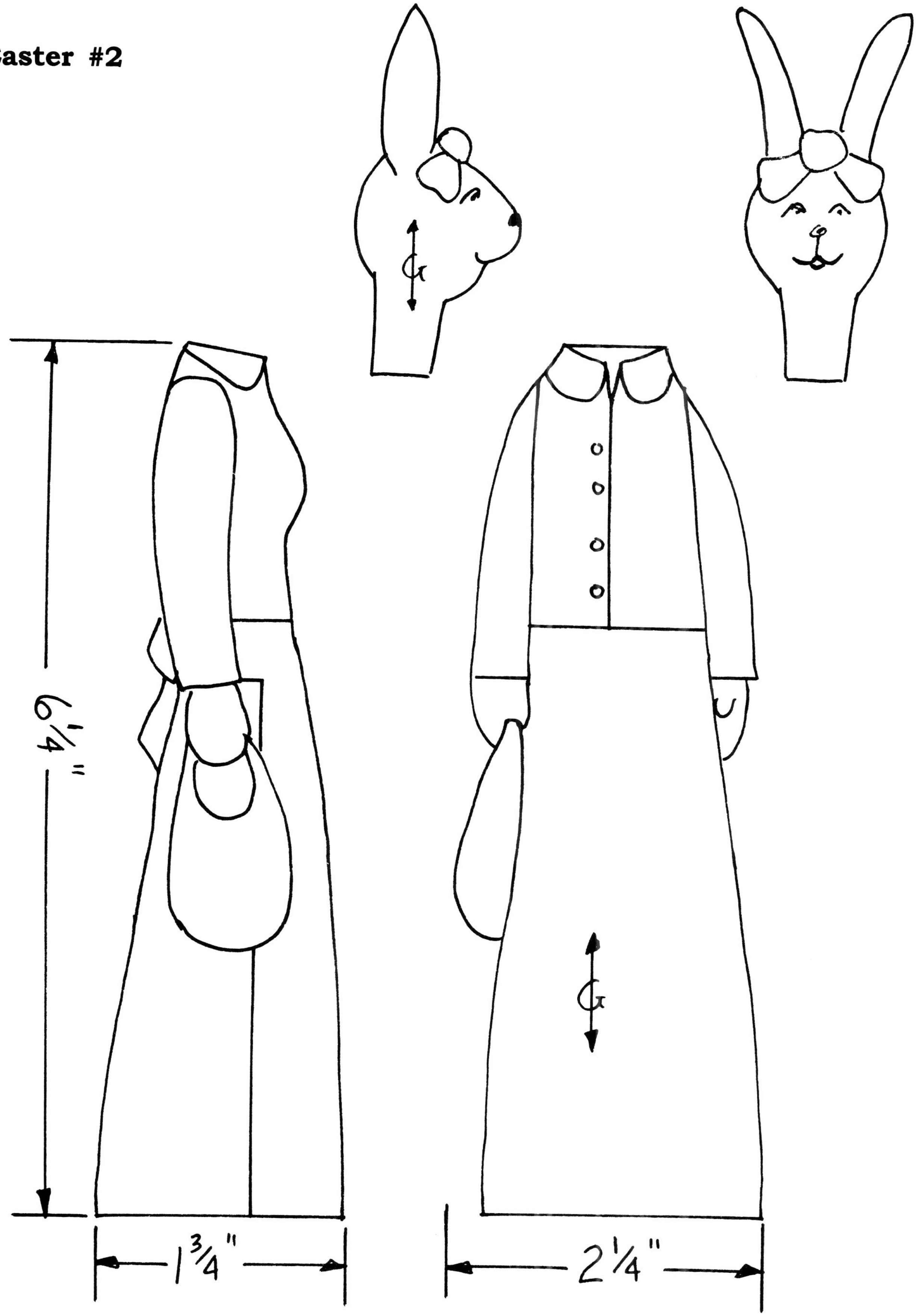

Easter #3

Carve body first. Then, measure distance between the hands (paws). Adjust the rough size of the egg to fit this dimension before sawing it out. Carve the egg so it just fits between the paws.

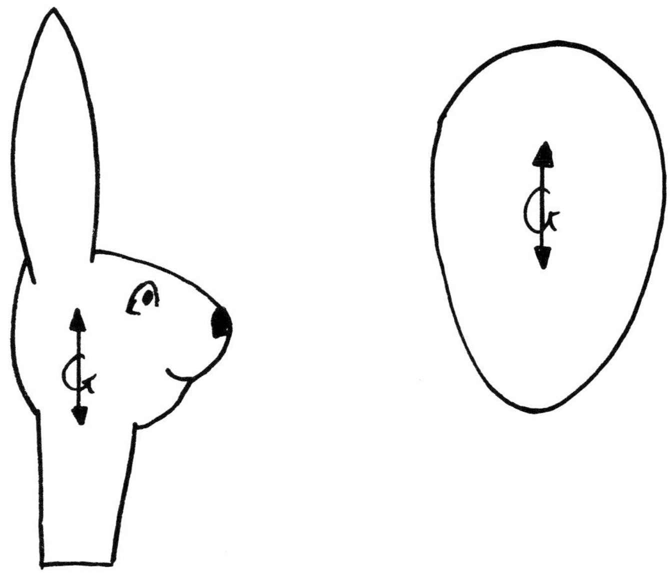

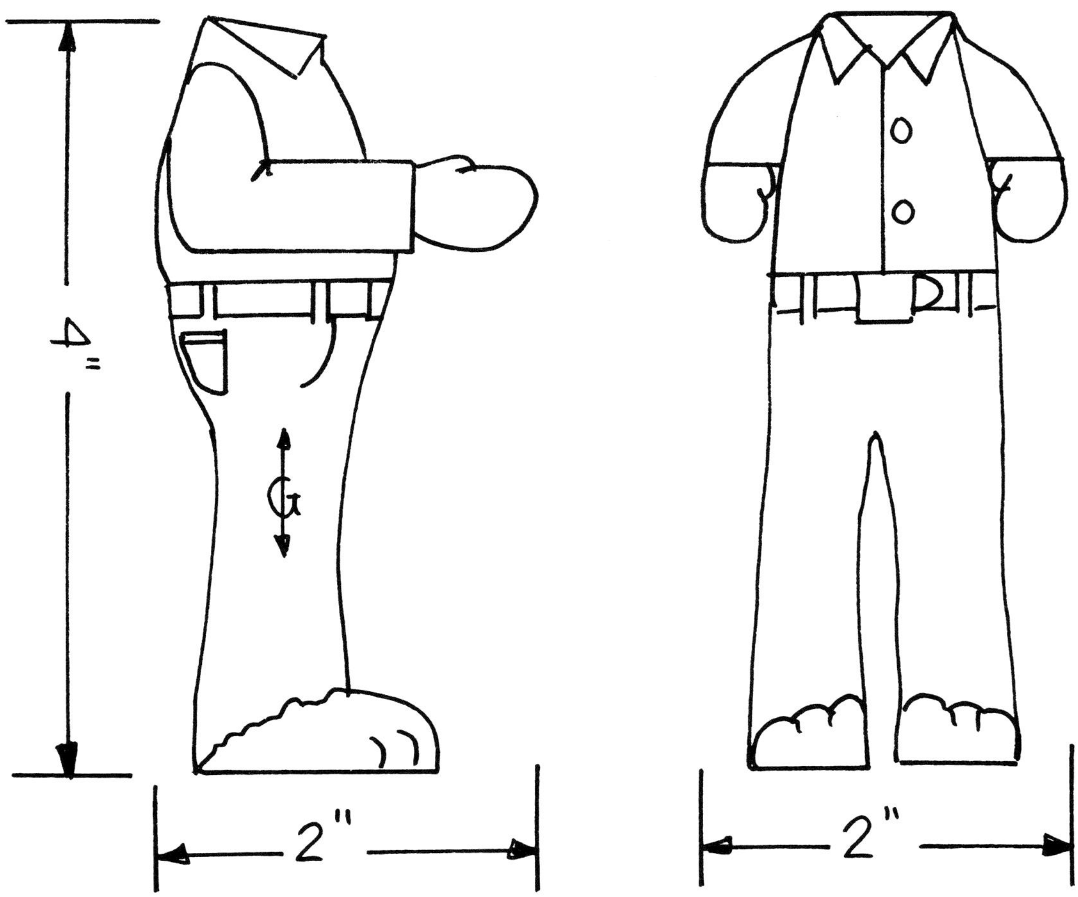

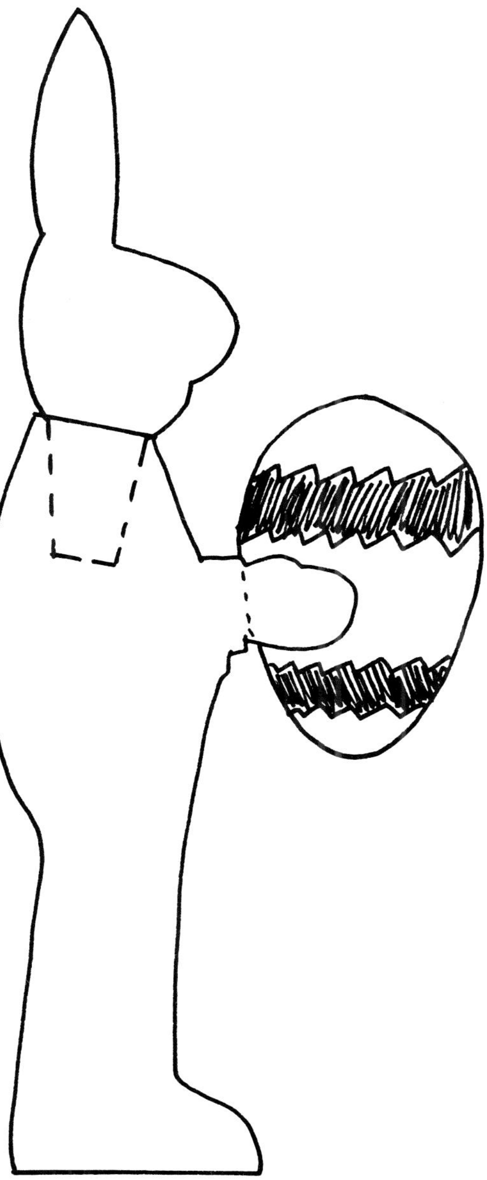

Christmas #2

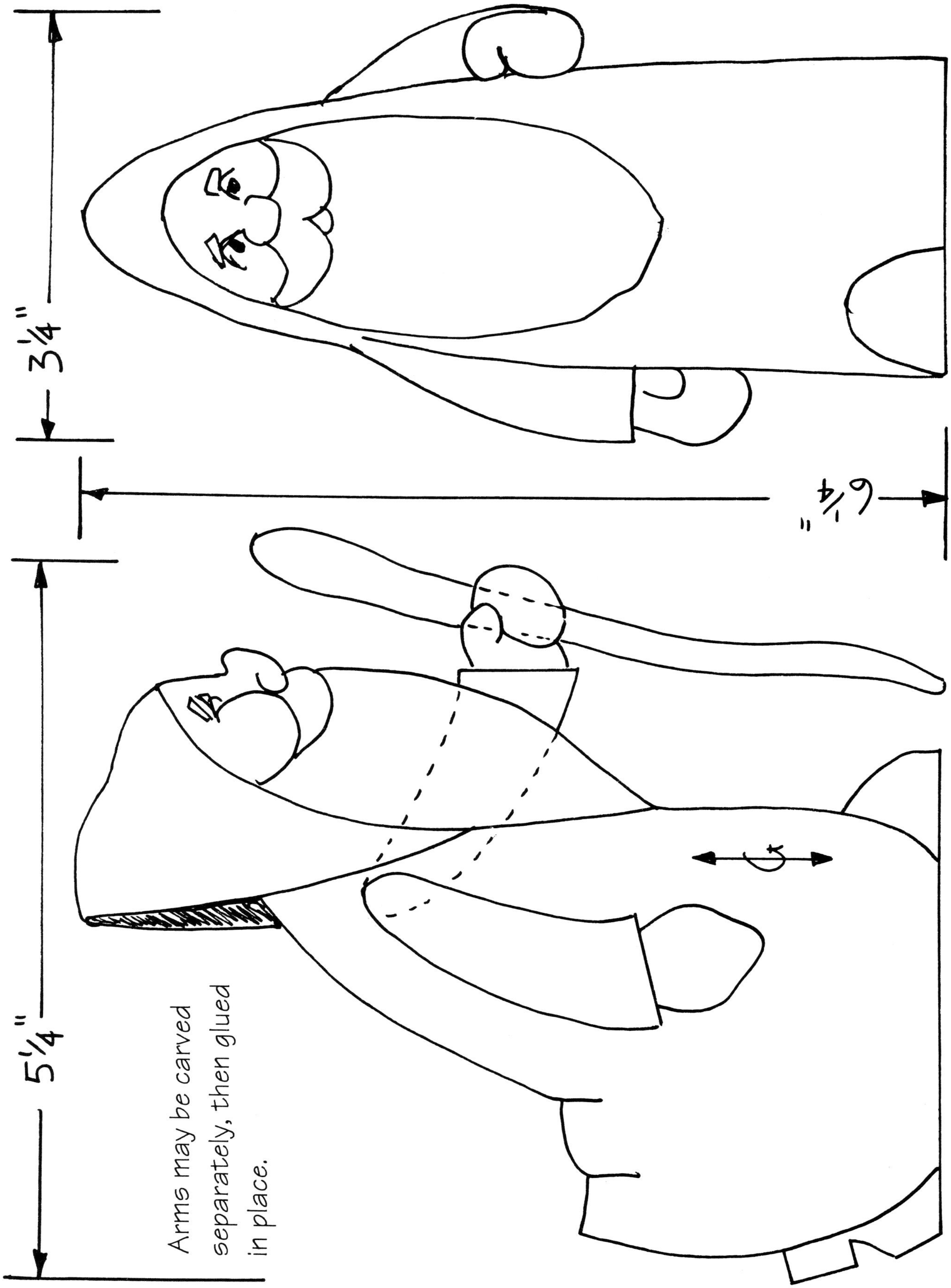

Christmas #3

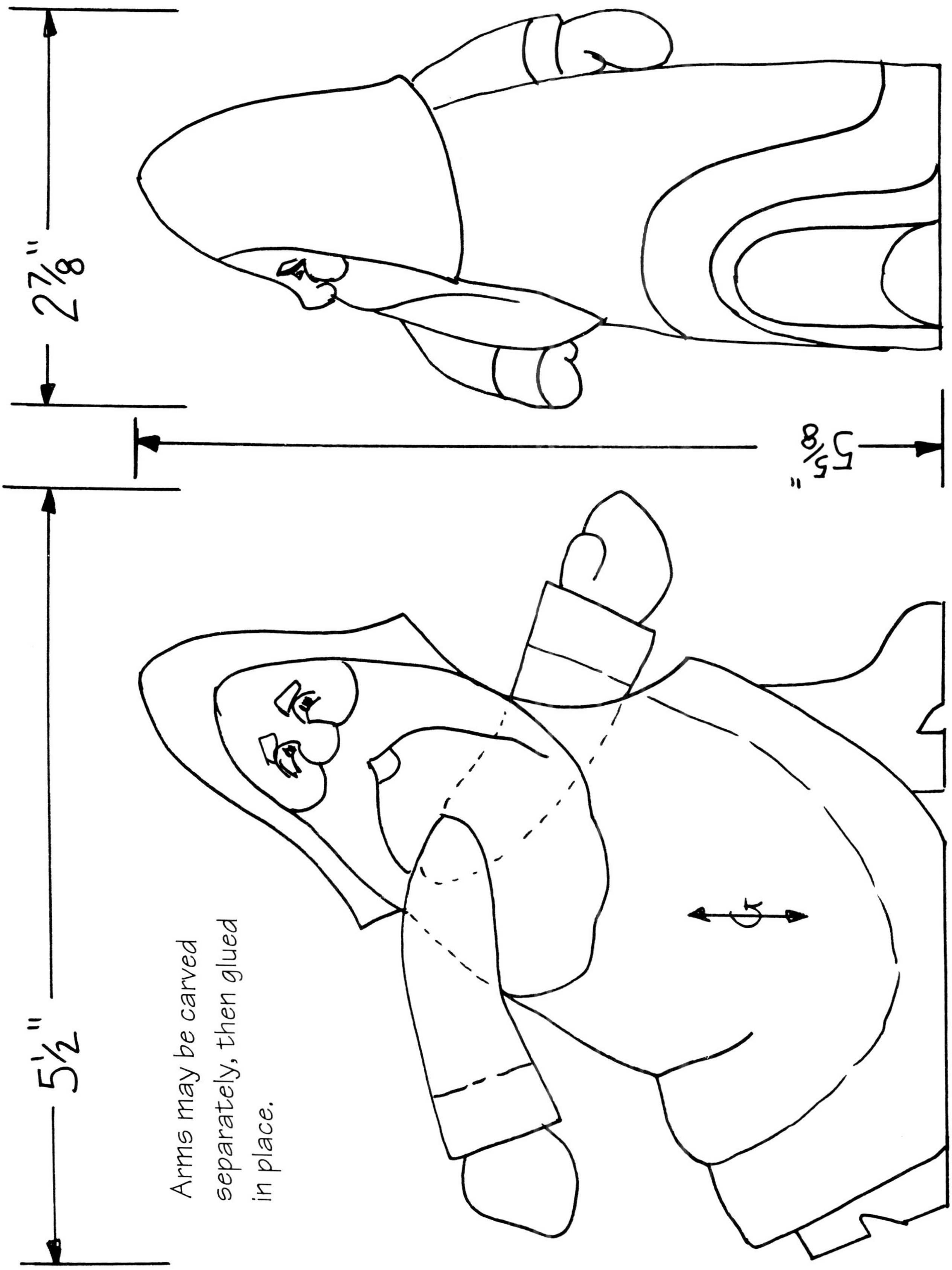
2 7/8"
5 5/8"
5 1/2"
Arms may be carved separately, then glued in place.

Christmas #4

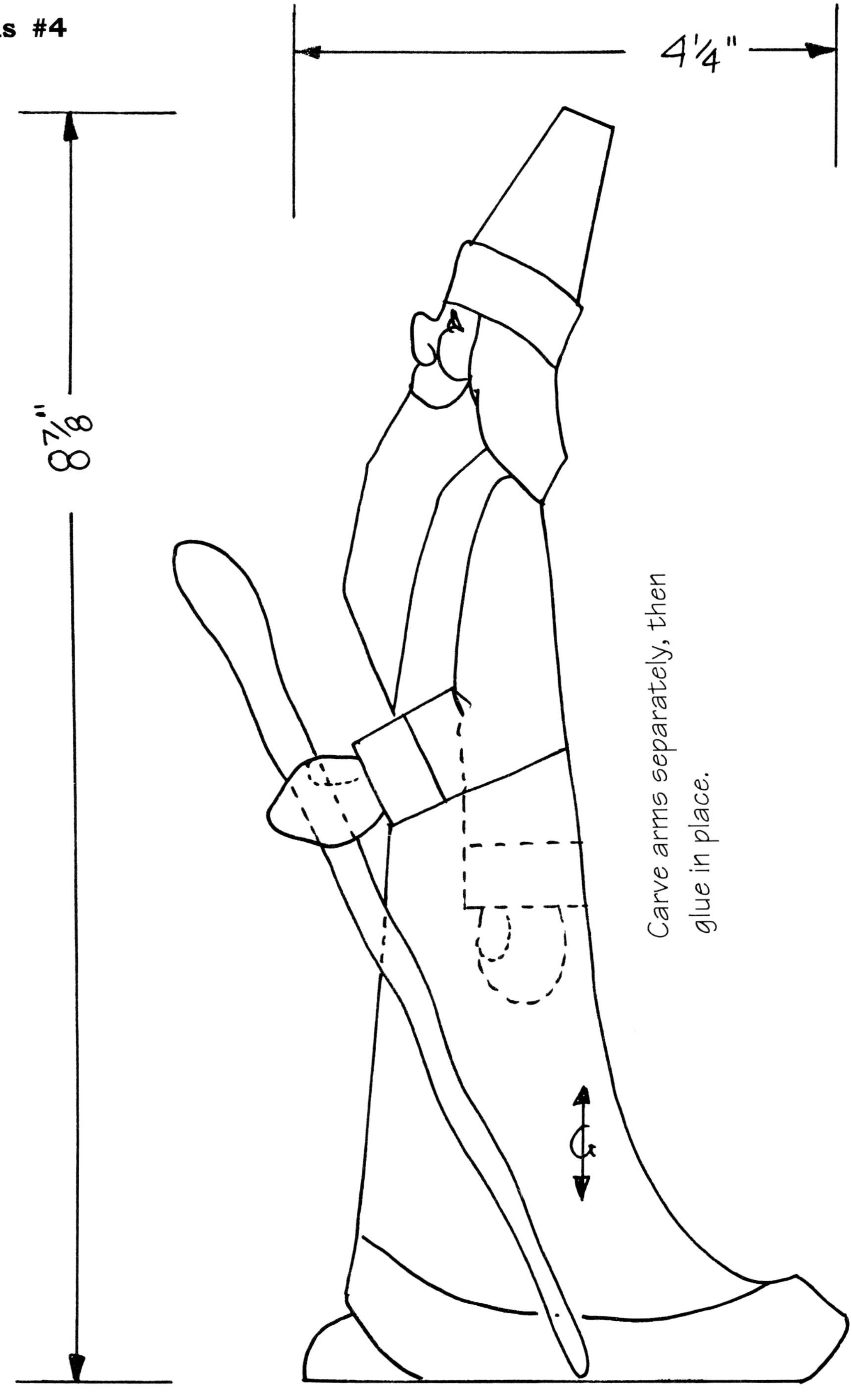

Christmas #5

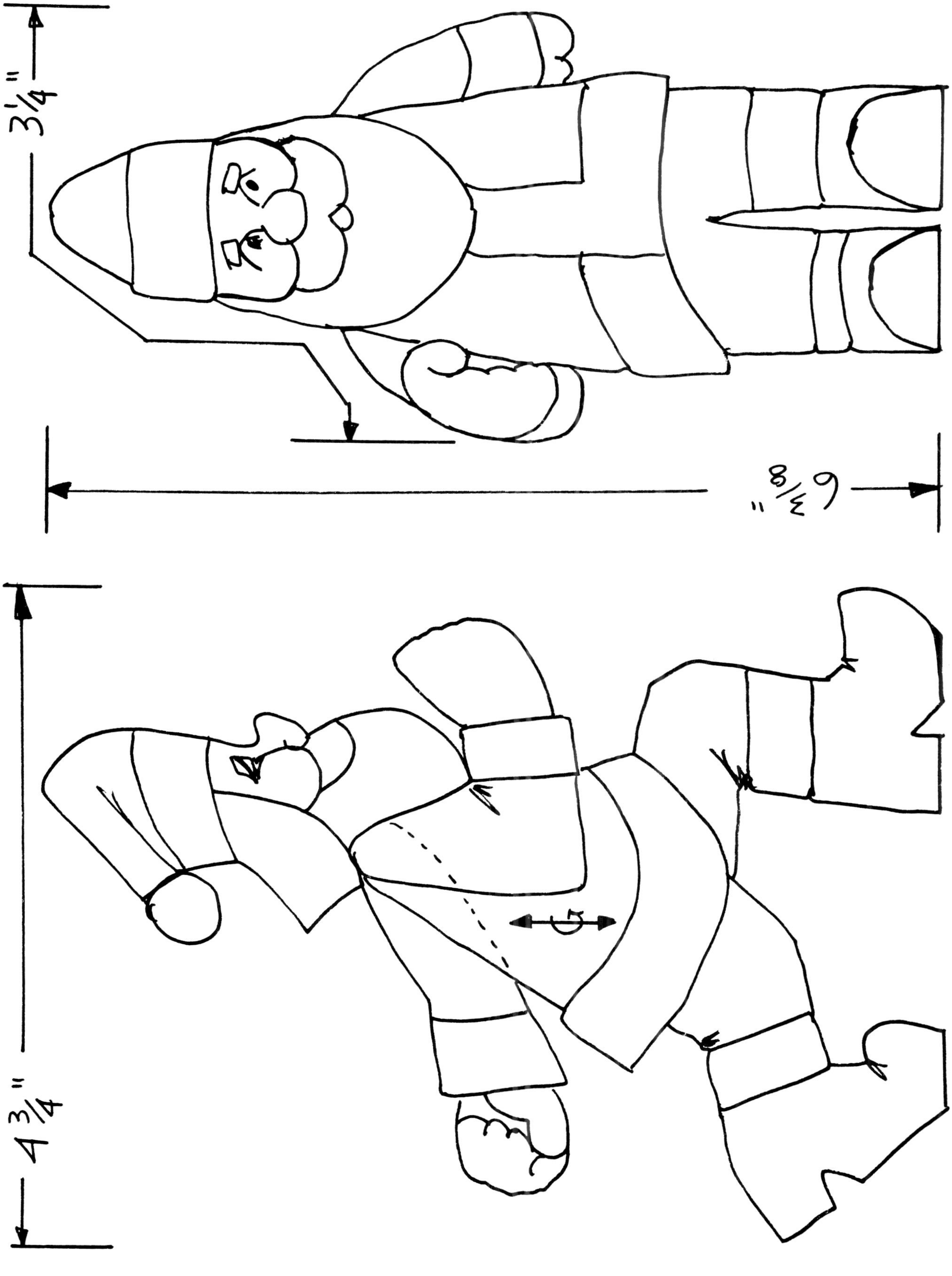

Candy cane main body is made from a 3/16" diameter wooden dowel. Cane head is made from a scrap piece of wood. Glue it to the body, then carve it to blend with the body. Drill a hole through the hand at the approximate angle indicated so the cane will fit through it and rest on Santa's shoulder.

Valentine's Day #1

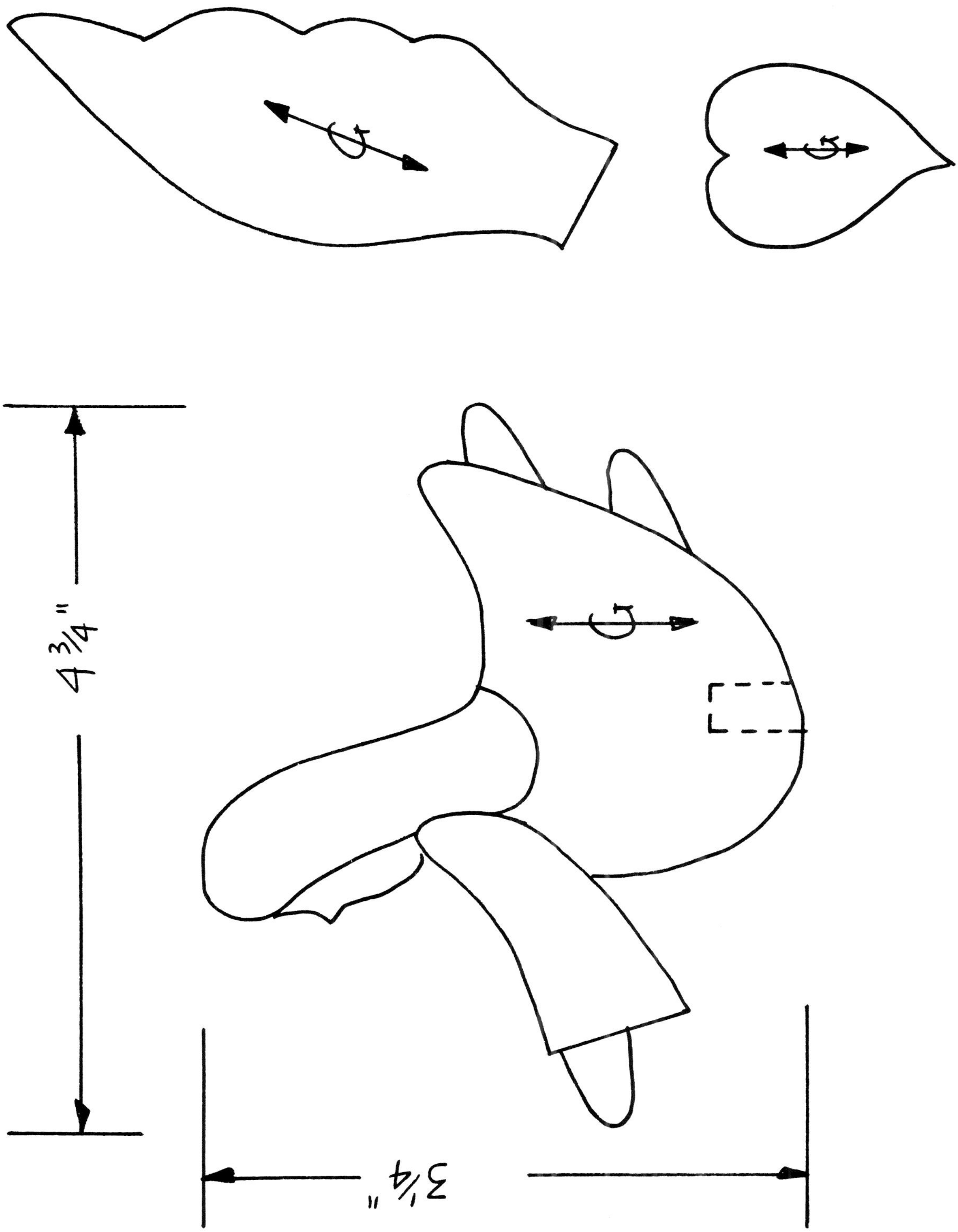

After carving angel, adjust the heart thickness to just fit between the hands.

Make a base of your choice and connect the angel to it with a section of wooden dowel as indicated.

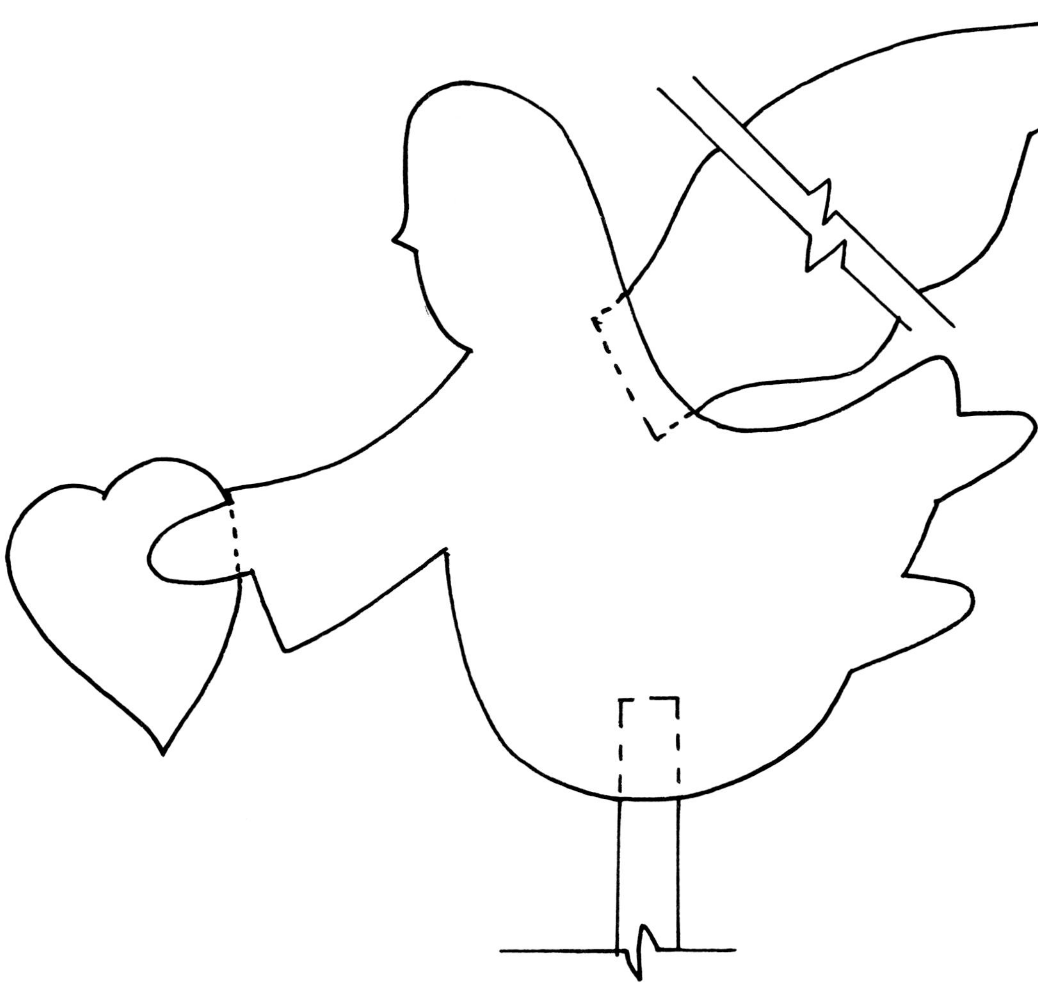

Valentine's Day #2

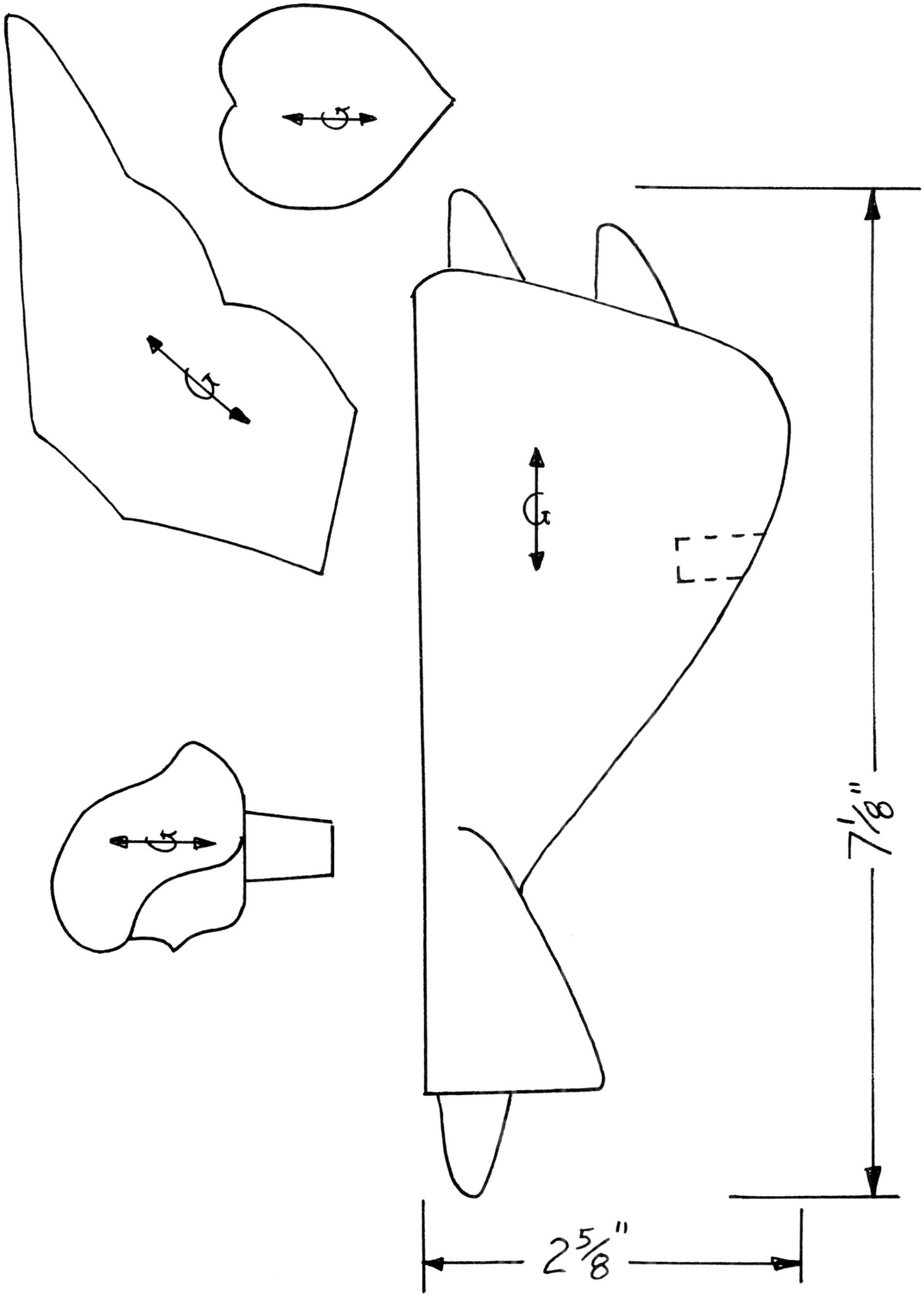

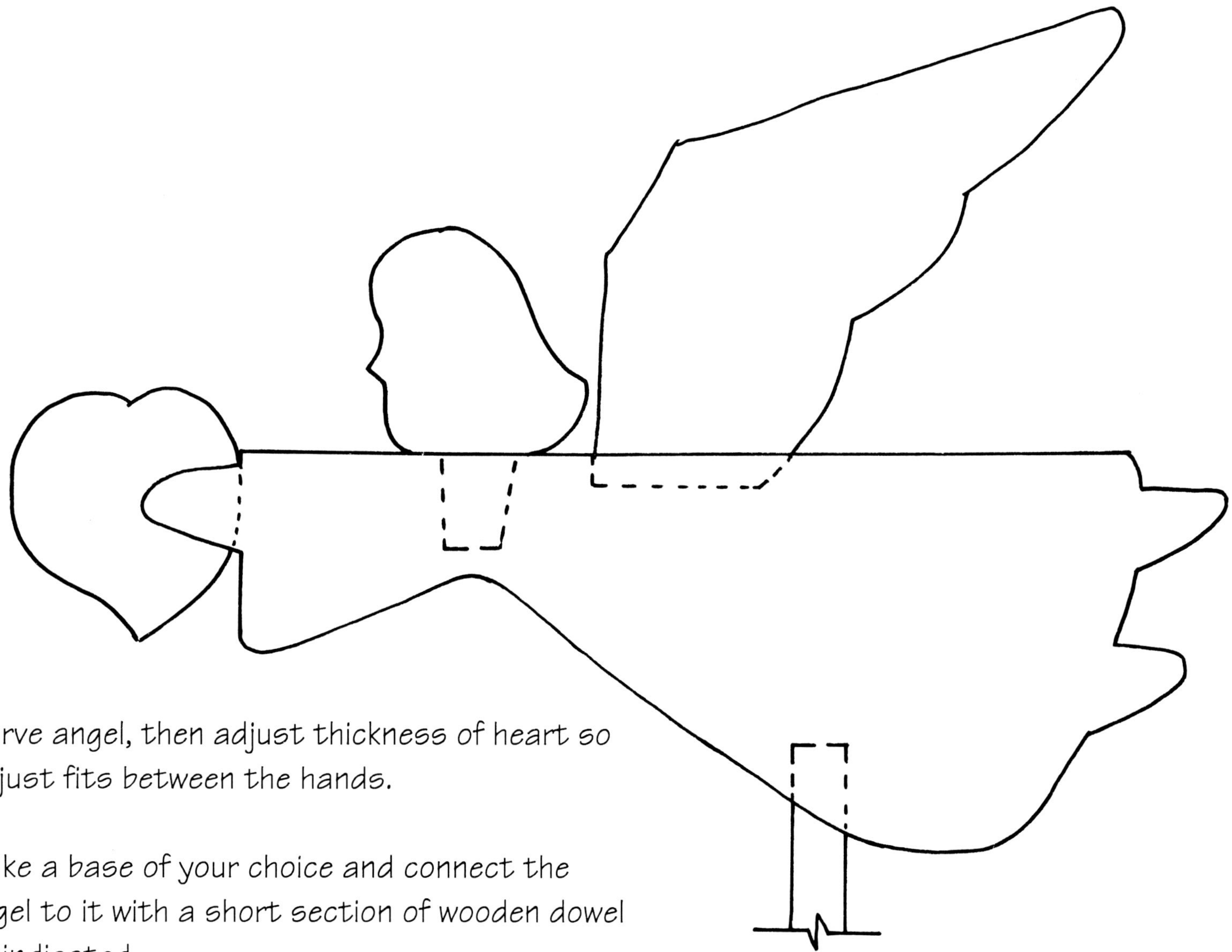

Carve angel, then adjust thickness of heart so it just fits between the hands.

Make a base of your choice and connect the angel to it with a short section of wooden dowel as indicated.

Valentine's Day #3

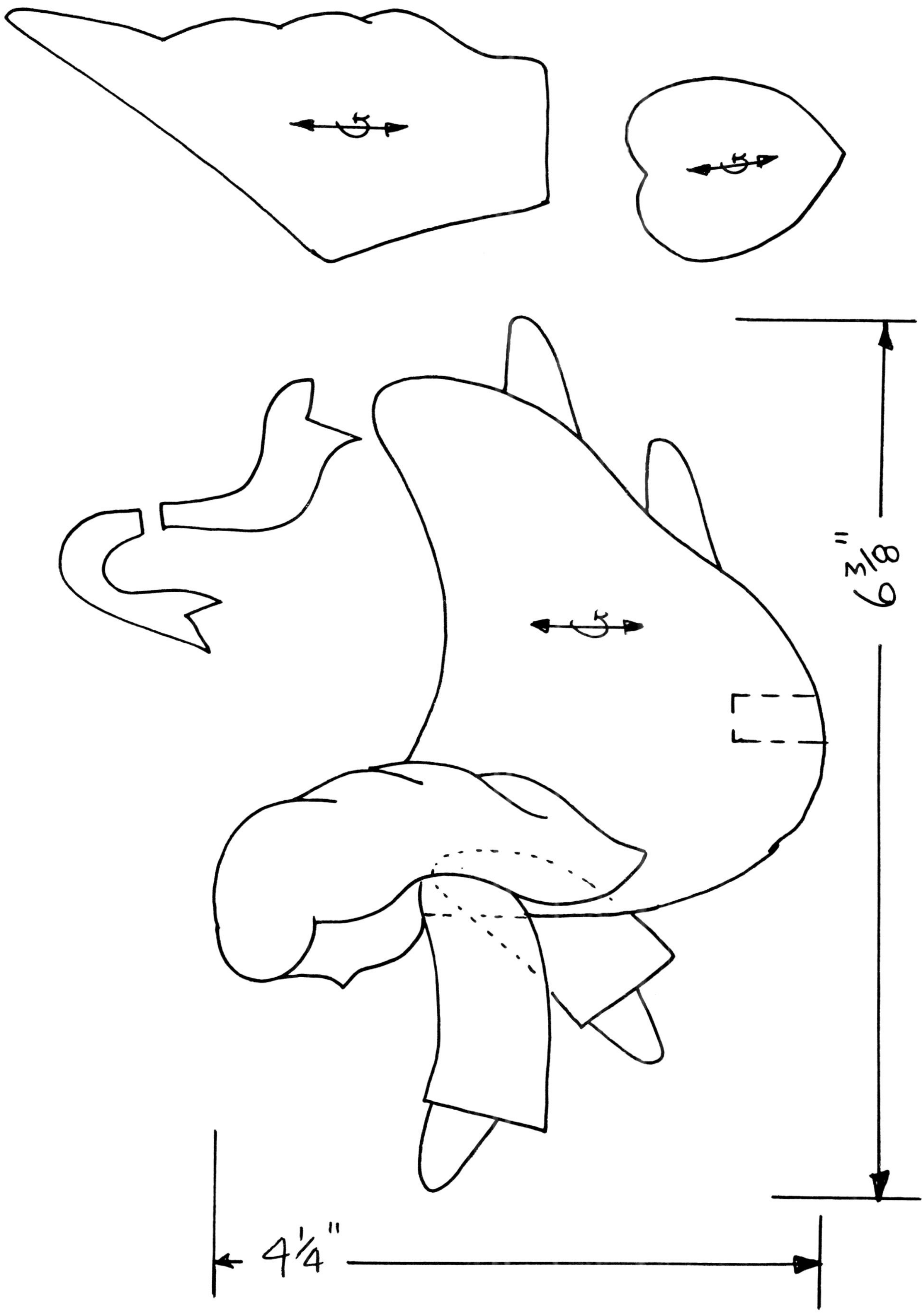

Carve the inside of the hand flat so the heart can be glued to it. If desired, you may carve a thumb and fingers on the hand. If so, saw the heart from thin wood so it fits in place.

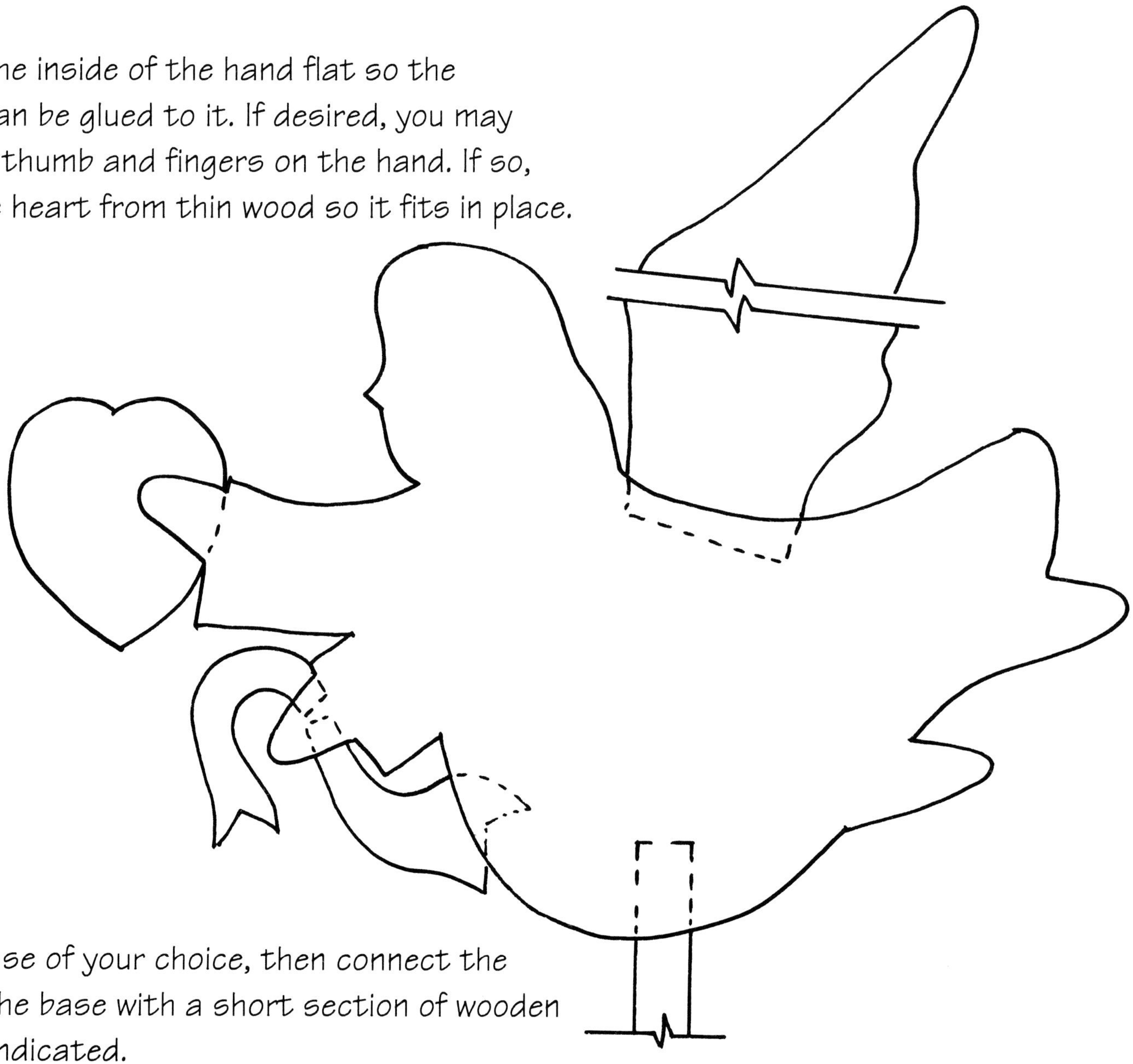

The ribbon is made in two pieces. Glue them in holes drilled in the hand.

Make a base of your choice, then connect the angel to the base with a short section of wooden dowel as indicated.

Hand Studies

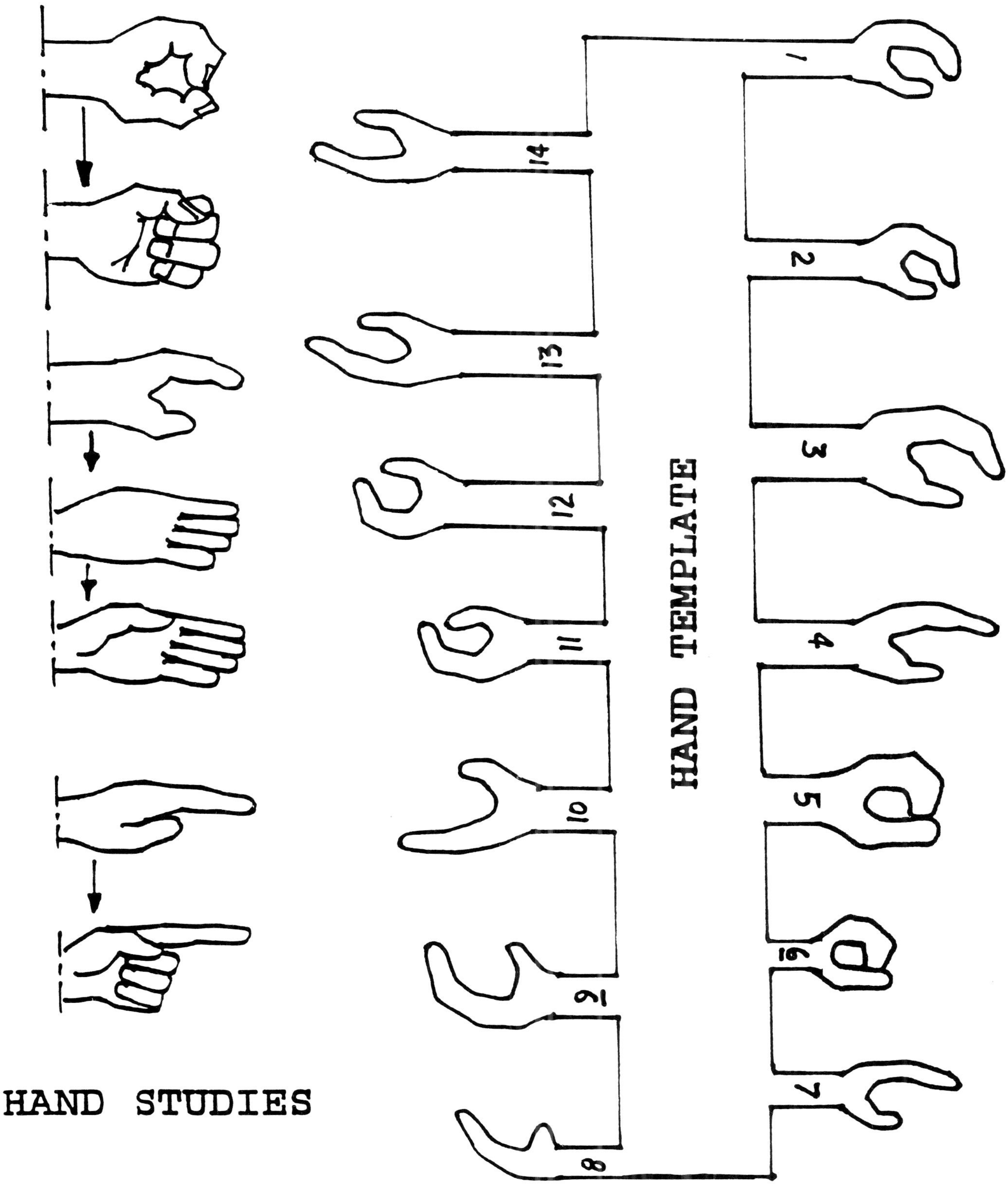

Gouge Reference Chart

Reprinted with the permission of Woodcraft Supply Corp.

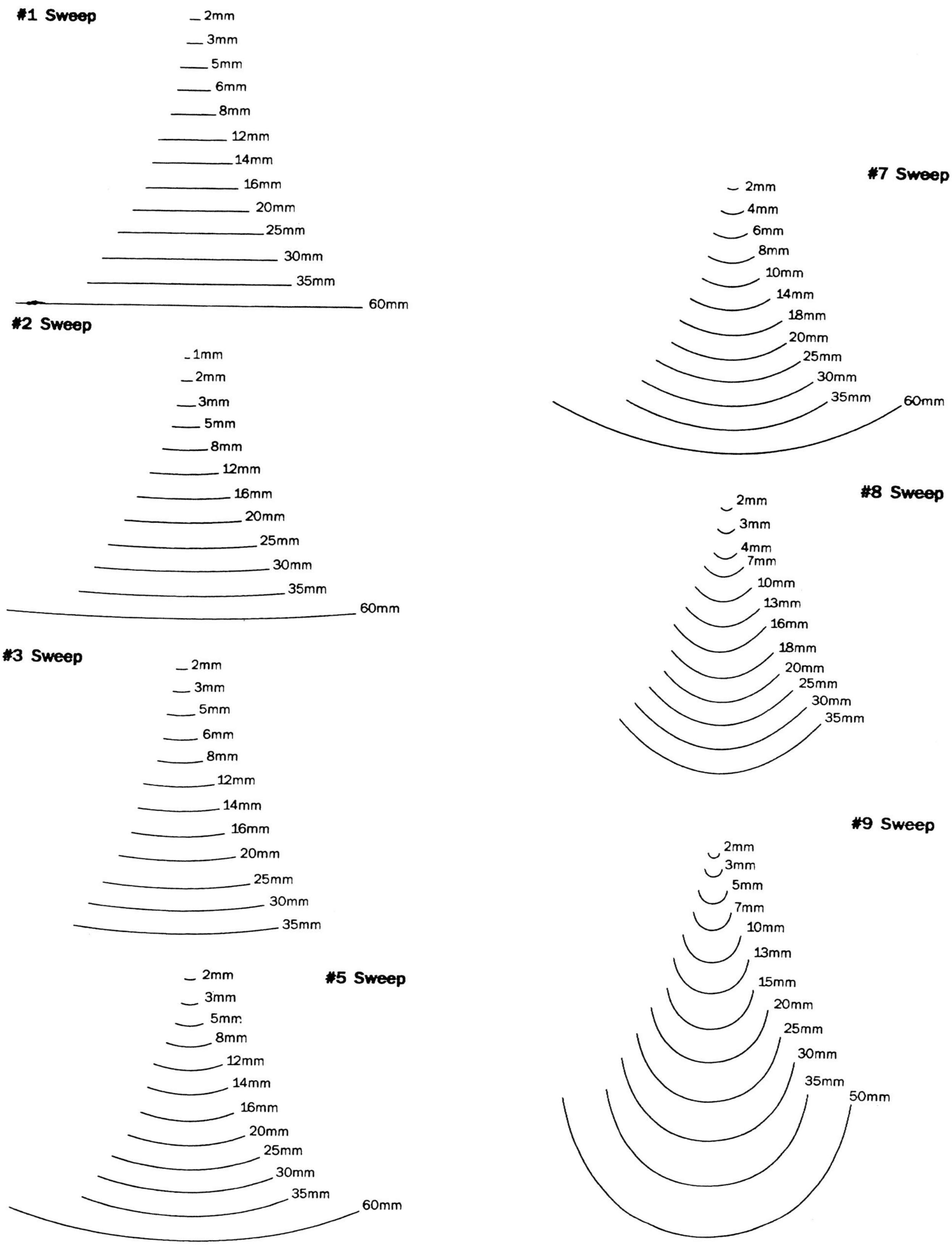

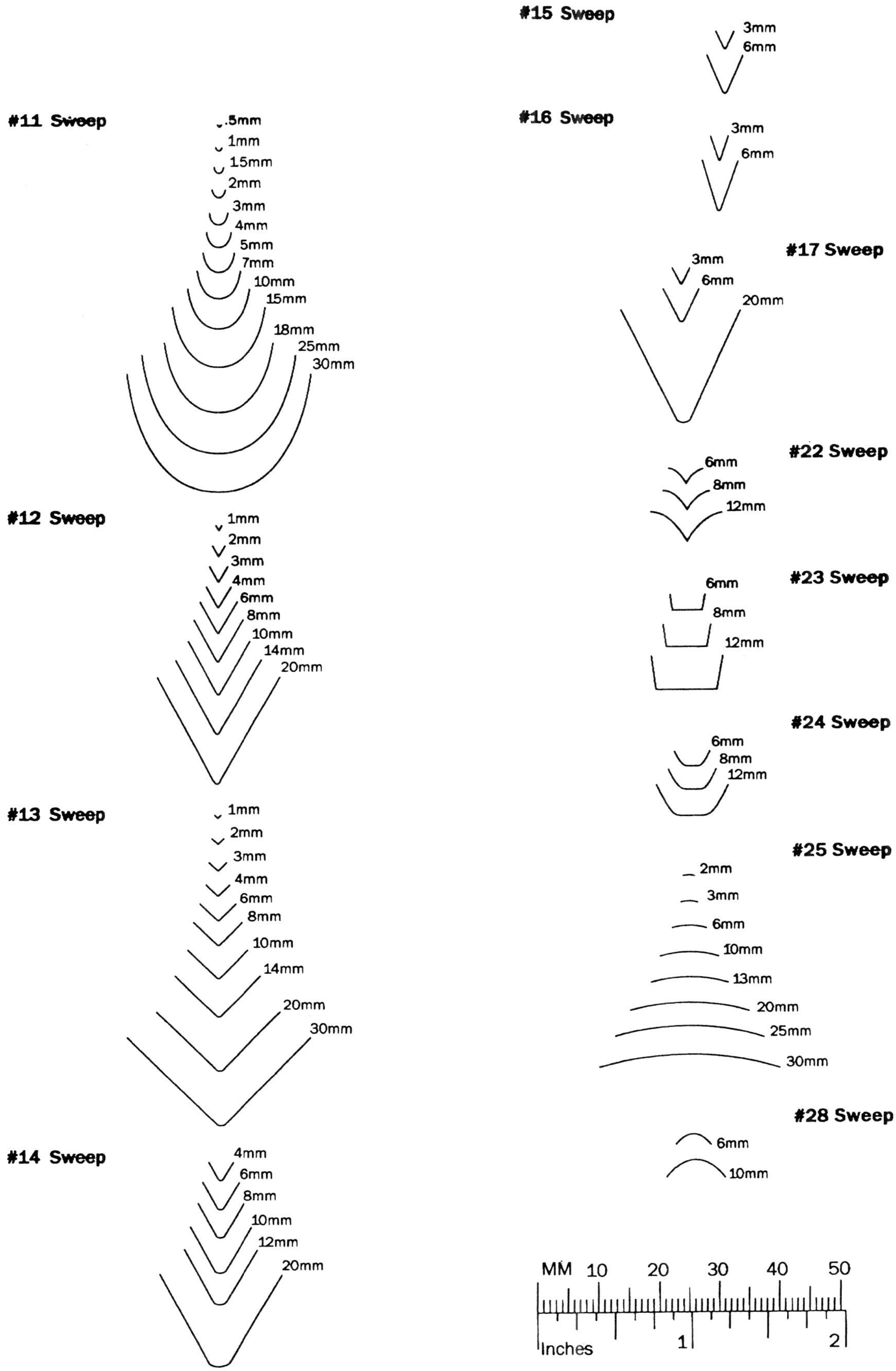
#11 Sweep
.5mm
1mm
1.5mm
2mm
3mm
4mm
5mm
7mm
10mm
15mm
18mm
25mm
30mm
#12 Sweep
1mm
2mm
3mm
4mm
6mm
8mm
10mm
14mm
20mm
#13 Sweep
1mm
2mm
3mm
4mm
6mm
8mm
10mm
14mm
20mm
30mm
#14 Sweep
4mm
6mm
8mm
10mm
12mm
20mm
#15 Sweep
3mm
6mm
#16 Sweep
3mm
6mm
#17 Sweep
3mm
6mm
20mm
#22 Sweep
6mm
8mm
12mm
#23 Sweep
6mm
8mm
12mm
#24 Sweep
6mm
8mm
12mm
#25 Sweep
2mm
3mm
6mm
10mm
13mm
20mm
25mm
30mm
#28 Sweep
6mm
10mm
MM 10 20 30 40 50
Inches 1 2

More Schiffer Titles

Santimals: Carving with Tom Wolfe Tom Wolfe; *text written with and photography by Douglas Congdon-Martin.* Santimals capture all the charm of the season in a new and delightful way. Tom takes the reader step-by-step through the carving of the raccoon Santimal, from the pattern to the painting. Each step is clearly illustrated with a full-color photograph and helpful description. Other Santimals include a goose, a hound dog, a duck, a pig, a mouse, a fox, and a bear.
Size 8 1/2" x 11" 64 pp.
ISBN: 0-88740-440-5 soft cover $12.95

Carving the Nativity with Helen Gibson In this wonderful new book an old tradition is shared with today's carvers. Helen takes the reader step-by-step through the delicate carving process of one of the creche figures, with clear color photography illustrating each technique. Patterns and complete views for the Mary, Joseph, three Wisemen, three Shepherds, and the baby in the manger are included.
Size: 8 1/2" x 11" 64 pp.
ISBN: 0-88740-438-3 soft cover $12.95

Helen Gibson Carves the Animals of the Nativity Helen Gibson. *Text written with and photography by Douglas Congdon-Martin.* Helen completes the nativity scene with the camels, sheep, cattle, and donkeys. Helen has a highly detailed style of carving that is perfect for this subject. The reader is lead step-by-step through the process of carving one of the animals. Clear color photographs illustrate every cut. A gallery of the other animals and patterns help the carver complete the set.
Size: 8 1/2" x 11" 250 color photos, patterns 64 pp.
ISBN: 0-88740-544-4 soft cover $12.95

A Folk Carved Nativity Donna Hefty *with photography by Marc Hefty.* Carving that is approachable and simple for all ages. Not only are there eleven highly defined patterns, but Donna will take you step-by-step through the process of both carving and painting. Each step is illustrated with a color photograph and an easy-to-follow description of the technique. A gallery shows the finished figures.The result is a wonderful project for carvers of all skill levels.
Size: 8 1/2" x 11" 64 pp.
Over 250 color photographs 11 patterns
ISBN: 0-88740-881-8 soft cover $12.95

Angel Carving Ron Ransom. Instructions for carving and painting appealing wooden angel figures with ease and humor. With many color and black-and-white illustrations of the creative steps, the book presents numerous different angel designs as weathervanes, Christmas ornaments, and free-standing figures of appealing and frequently whimsical personalities. The instructions encourage all to try.
Size: 8 1/2 " x 11" 80 pp.
143 b/w photographs 49 color photographs
ISBN: 0-88740-147-3 soft cover $9.95

Carving Santas with Special Interests Ron Ransom *with photography by George A. Clark.* Seven new step-by-step Santa projects from Ron Ransom. These Santas have special interests including golf, fishing, and skiing, among others. As always Ron Ransom makes the carving easy, interesting, and fun.
Size: 8 1/2" x 11" Full color photographs 64 pp.
ISBN:: 0-88740-328-X soft cover $12.95

Mini-Cheers©: Carving Miniature Santas Ron Ransom. *Text written with and photography by Jeffrey B. Snyder* Santa "Mini-Cheers"© answer the wood carver's perennial question, "What can I do with all of these basswood scraps?" Here are six patterns and instructions for carving three miniature Santas and a larger Santa holding a snowman, all carved in an "Old World" style, with simplicity and character. Ron skillfully guides the carver through each project with straight-forward, step-by-step directions, color illustrations, and a bit of humor. A gallery is included.
Size: 8 1/2" x 11" 64 pp.
Over 260 color photographs 6 patterns
ISBN: 0-88740-824-9 soft cover $12.95

Santa Carving Ron Ransom. These figures are unique creations of author-carver Ron Ransom. *Santa Carving* offers instructions for three specific versions of Santa Claus and many other variations, as well as painting instructions. Mr. Ransom's illustrations serve as an impetus for the carver to approach his own work with freedom. His "Old World Santas'' are great symbols of happiness and goodness.
Size: 8 1/2" x 11" 46 pp.
20 color photos; 57 b/w photos 5 drawings
ISBN: 0-88740-107-4 soft cover $8.95

Old St. Nick Carving: Classic Santas from Wood David Sabol. *Text written with and photography by Jeffrey B. Snyder.* David Sabol takes the reader through each step from wood blank to finished carving with clear, step-by-step instructions and color illustrations. Patterns are provided for six classic Santas in a variety of poses and for the venerable Mrs. Claus as well. A color gallery shows each of the finished patterns to fire the imagination of every carver.
Size: 8 1/2" x 11" 64 pp.
Over 250 color photographs 7 patterns
ISBN: 0-7643-0039-3 soft cover $12.95

Santa Carving Ron Ransom. These figures are unique creations of author-carver Ron Ransom. *Santa Carving* offers instructions for three specific versions of Santa Claus and many other variations, as well as painting instructions. Mr. Ransom's illustrations serve as an impetus for the carver to approach his own work with freedom. His "Old World Santas'' are great symbols of happiness and goodness.
Size: 8 1/2" x 11" 46 pp.
20 color photos; 57 b/w photos 5 drawings
ISBN: 0-88740-107-4 soft cover $8.95